EASY **SINGER** STYLE

pattern-free
fashions & accessories

15 easy-sew projects that build skills, too

kate perri

Creative Publishing
international

Creative Publishing international

Copyright 2007
Creative Publishing international
18705 Lake Drive East
Chanhassen, Minnesota 55317
1-800-328-3895
www.creativepub.com
All rights reserved

President/CEO: Ken Fund
Vice President/Sales & Marketing: Peter Ackroyd
Executive Managing Editor: Barbara Harold
Acquisition Editor: Deborah Cannarella
Development Editor: Sharon Boerbon Hanson
Creative Director: Michele Lanci-Altomare
Art Director: Mary Rohl
Production Manager: Laura Hokkanen, Linda Halls
Cover and Book Design: Mary Rohl
Photo Stylist: Joanne Wawra
Photographers: Rudy Calin, Steve Galvin, Andrea Rugg
Page Layout: Lois Stanfield
Illustration: Deborah Pierce

Library of Congress Cataloging-in-Publication Data
Perri, Kate.
  Pattern-free fashions & accessories : 15 easy-sew projects that build
skills, too / Kate Perri.
      p. cm. — (Easy singer style)
  Branded by Singer At head of title:
Includes index.
  ISBN-13: 978-1-58923-312-6 (soft cover)
  ISBN-10: 1-58923-312-3 (soft cover)
  1. Machine sewing. I. Title. II. Title: At head of title:. III. Series.
  TT713.P43 2007
  646.2'044—dc22   2006032894

Printed in China
10 9 8 7 6 5 4 3 2 1

Due to differing conditions, materials, and skill levels, the publisher and various manufacturers disclaim any liability for unsatisfactory results or injury due to improper use of tools, materials, or information in this publication.

acknowledgments

Thank you to Aron, Dan, and Ben. I love you! Thanks to Susan Guagliumi for years of friendship, humor, and advice. Thanks to Nancy Rosenberger, owner of the Quilt Cottage (Mamaroneck, New York) for embroidery, friendship, notions, and tea. Thanks to Ben Pasternack for his T-shirt designs, stenciling, and patience. Thanks to Libby Hollahan, Madalyn Kozlow, Lisa Ihde Costa, Ellen Highsmith Silver, and my many friends for supporting me, sharing my excitement, and laughing at my jokes. Thanks to all the girls and boys in my classes, for testing patterns and being so creative.

Many thanks to all the suppliers for letting me play with their beautiful fabrics. It has been a pleasure to work with editor Deborah Cannarella. Her support and encouragement were always thoughtful and unflagging. Thank you, Creative Publishing international, for the opportunity to write about my lifelong passion.

about the author

Kate Perri teaches hand and machine sewing and quilting to middle-school-age boys and girls in after-school programs, camp programs, workshops, and private classes. She has developed a range of projects based on these experiences—and on kids' special requests. Kate has a BFA in Designer Crafts from the Maryland Institute College of Art in Baltimore. Visit her at www.kateperridesigns.com.

contents

welcome to sewing!

Whether you've never threaded a needle or you've only dabbled with sewing on your own, this is the place to discover the techniques and tricks to begin sewing successfully. Each project in this book teaches a skill or skills that you will use every time you sew. The first three projects offer explanations of hand-sewing. The comprehensive chapter on the sewing machine explains the parts and the functions of the machine, which you can refer to again and again. Best of all, you will learn to make great accessories, home decorating projects, and simple garments. Check out the chapter, "Change Your Clothes"—and before you know it, you'll be sorting through your closet looking for things to alter and embellish.

What could be better than displaying your own creativity and skill for your family and friends? You'll be amazed how people react when you're wearing the sensational silky prom wrap you made or when you present a photo pillow you created as a gift.

Picking and choosing fabrics, notions, and trims makes projects personal and unique. Tap into your creative side, and you will be exploring your unique vision for the rest of your life.

Have fun! You can sew it!

fabric facts

Shopping for fabric is exciting, but looking at the wide selection of choices can be overwhelming. Learning about fabric makes it easier to choose. The fabrics you'll need to make each project (and the amounts you'll need) are provided with the project instructions, but here are some basics to get you started.

Width and Length

Selvage refers to the finished edge on each side of the fabric. Fabric width is the measurement from selvage edge to selvage edge.

Apparel fabrics are best for making clothes. They come 45" (115 cm) or 60" (150 cm) wide. Fabrics for home décor usually run 54" (138 cm) wide. Quilters often use calico-weight cotton, which runs 42" (107 cm) to 44" (112 cm) wide.

For clothing, choose lightweight fabrics, such as cottons; specialty fabrics, like silks, satins, and taffetas; or heavier fabrics, like denim and corduroy. When making pillows, curtains, and upholstery, choose gauzy fabrics, heavy cottons, brocades, and tapestries.

Grain

The grain of the fabric runs parallel to the selvages. Grain is important when you're planning any type of sewing project. Commercial patterns indicate the direction of the grain with an arrow. Before cutting fabric, lay the pattern pieces to position the arrows in the same direction as the grain (with the grain). When you match the grain, your sewn project pieces will hang correctly.

Right or Wrong?

Project instructions refer to the "right side" and the "wrong side" of the fabric. The right side is on the outside of your finished project or garment. The wrong side is the other side.

The wrong side of a printed fabric often looks slightly faded. Fabrics with a nap, such as velvets and corduroy, also appear noticeably different on their wrong (flatter) side. Brocades and tapestries have a different pattern on the wrong side.

It's not always easy to find the right side of a fabric. Some solids, cottons, plaids, and stripes look the same on both sides. When working with look-alike sides, choose one as the right side and lay out your pattern. Cut out the pattern pieces, but before removing the paper patterns, mark the top side of the fabric with a safety pin, a piece of tape, or a chalk mark. Be sure to mark every pattern piece. Treat the sides you marked as the wrong sides of the fabric.

Preparation and Care

Shrinking affects the fit, size, and shape of the finished project. If you plan to clean the finished project or garment by washing, wash and dry the fabric before cutting and sewing it. That way, if the fabric shrinks, it will have done so before your project is constructed. Also, excess dye rinses out in the first wash so you avoid turning the rest of your laundry a different color! Iron the fabric as soon as it comes out of the dryer.

Press as You Go

If you iron your fabric as you sew, your projects will have such a professional look no one will ever guess they're homemade. It's also easier to cut wrinkle-free fabric and to sew across seams that have been pressed open. Pressing individual pieces as you assemble them is easier than pressing them after they are stitched together.

There are three ways to use the iron: pressing, ironing, and steaming. Pressing means applying heat and pressure by putting the iron down firmly and then lifting it off the fabric. This method is good for flattening seams and bonding fusible facings. Ironing means sliding the iron back and forth to smooth out wrinkles. Steaming means to hold the iron just over the fabric and let the water vapors of the steam penetrate the fibers. Steaming also relaxes wrinkles and helps you to

gently shape fabric. When sewing garments and home-decorating projects, you usually press fabric.

After sewing seams, press them open with the tip of the iron. This method smoothes and flattens the seam from the inside to give a crisp seam on the outside. Make a habit of pressing seams open as you sew them. Press as you measure and as you turn under edges, hems, and casings, and you will sew accurately and smoothly.

Be careful when using an iron. Never leave it face down on the ironing board—not even for a minute. Not only could you burn the fabric, you could start a fire. Always unplug the iron after you have finished working with it.

here's a hint!

Before buying fabric, always check the label or ask the salesperson if the fabric is washable. Some apparel fabrics and home-decorating fabrics must be professionally dry-cleaned, which can be expensive or impractical.

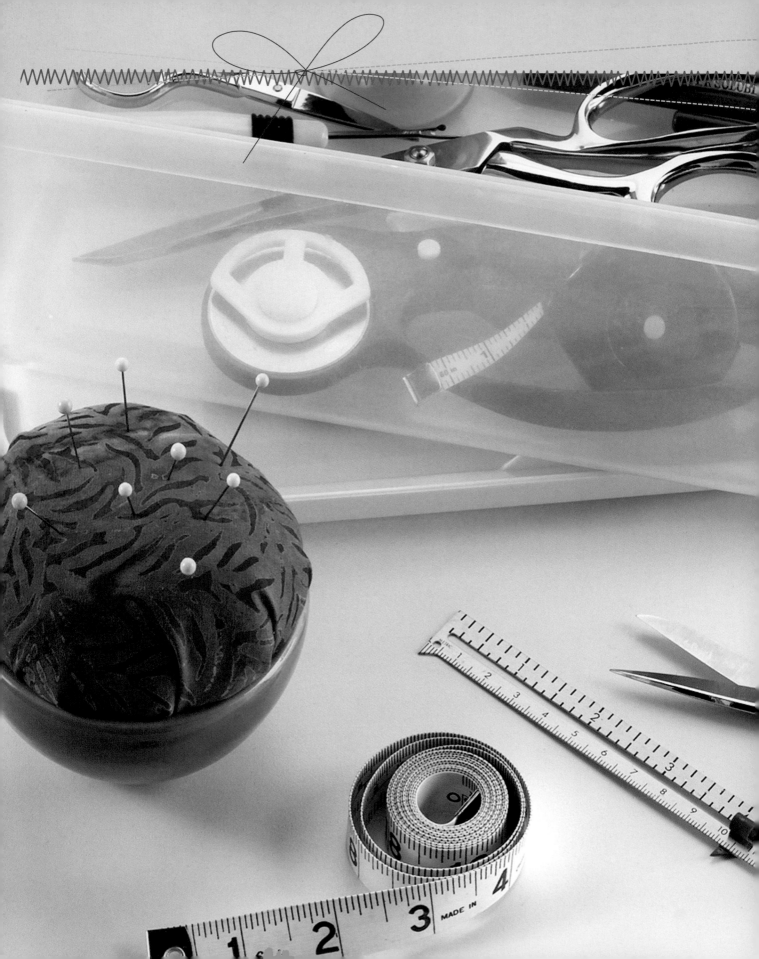

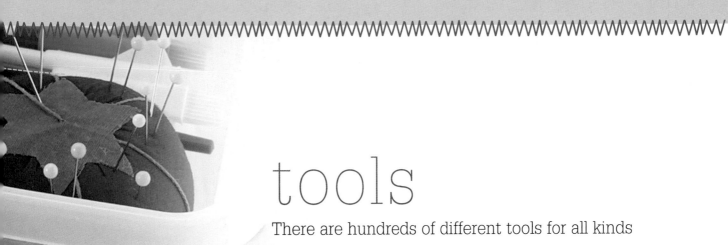

tools

There are hundreds of different tools for all kinds of sewing, but there are really only a few basic supplies that all sewers need. Think about where to store your tools. A sewing basket or a plastic or cardboard shoebox work well. Your container doesn't need to be fancy, just portable—preferably with a lid. Return your tools to the box when you finish to keep them from being damaged or misplaced. You'll be organized and ready to sew when inspiration hits.

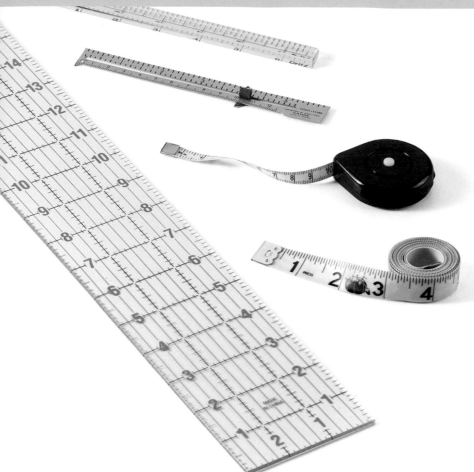

Marking

Marking tools are the pens and pencils of sewing. All during the sewing process, you need to mark the fabric, temporarily, with seam allowances, construction details, and the placement of trims and buttons. Never use pencils, pens, or markers designed for writing.

Always test a fabric marking tool on a scrap piece of your fabric to ensure that the marks can be easily seen. Usually, you want the marks to appear only on one side of the fabric.

Easy-to-use chalk dispensing tools leave a precise line that brushes off easily. These tools are great when you are marking fabric just before going to the sewing machine to stitch. Some chalk markers have a waxy ingredient that allows the mark to last longer on the fabric. Tailor's chalk is a chalk wedge that works well on most things—but test it on a bit of your fabric to make sure it doesn't leave a mark when ironed.

Measuring

Sewing, like any kind of construction, requires accurate measuring for a successful look and fit.

A flexible tape measure is handy for taking body measurements, working with patterns, measuring fabric, and checking measurements as you sew. Look for a fiberglass or plastic tape measure 60" (153 cm) long. Most tape measures are marked with both inches and centimeters. Purchase a rigid, clear acrylic sewing ruler with lines and grids (they come in many shapes and sizes). It is a "must have" tool for cutting fabric with a rotary cutter, but is also useful for many other measuring tasks. Use it for marking accurate cutting lines and seam allowances directly onto fabric. You'll need a yardstick when measuring hems from the floor.

A seam gauge is a thin and rigid 6" (15 cm) metal tool with a sliding marker in the center. Use the gauge to check the seam allowance at the sewing machine or to make an even fold or a hem.

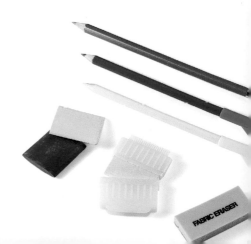

Seam Ripper, Pins, and Pincushions

A seam ripper is an essential tool. You will have to rip out stitches at some point! With a seam ripper, you can easily pick out a few stitches or a whole line. (For instructions on how to use a seam ripper, see page 99.)

All-purpose dressmaker pins are a medium length and good for general sewing. Colored heads make pins easy to see and grab.

If there are pins and needles, there must be a pincushion! Every sewing box needs at least one. Pincushions come in every shape and size, from *Pretty Pincushions*

(page 24) to the classic tomato shape. There are pincushions to place on your sewing machine or to wear on your wrist, and even pincushions with magnets (very helpful if you drop a pin or lots of pins on the floor).

Shears and Scissors

Even though we all use the term "scissors," scissors and shears are different tools. Sewing scissors, good for clipping seams and trimming, have two round holes for the fingers and are about 6" (15 cm) long. Shears have a round hole for the thumb and a larger oval for two or three fingers. They are longer than scissors, too—usually 8" to 10" (20.5 to 25.5 cm) long. Look for a pair

with bent handles, which allow the blade to stay on the table and the fabric to lie flat while you cut. Use sewing shears to cut fabric of all weights.

Embroidery scissors are sharp and small (less than 6" [15 cm] long) with two narrow pointed blades. They are great for hand-sewing and for trimming threads.

Every household has a junk drawer with a pair of scissors in it. This is not the place to find or

to keep sewing scissors! Tools used for cutting fabric should only be used for cutting fabric. Cutting paper or cardboard dulls and ruins the tools and your fabric. Store shears and scissors with your sewing notions and other tools. Invest in the best quality possible. Take care of them, and they will last for years. Lefties, look for left-handed scissors and shears, which are designed just for you.

Rotary Cutting Tools

Rotary cutting is a system for cutting with a rotary cutter, cutting mat, and clear acrylic ruler. As these tools are always used together, they often come in kits. Rotary cutting allows quick, accurate cutting of geometric shapes. Many accessory and home decorating projects start with simple squares and rectangles. With rotary cutting, these pieces can be cut to size without the need for paper patterns.

The rotary cutter is a rolling razor blade—and extremely sharp. It comes with a retractable cover to protect the blade (and your fingers) when not in use. Make it a habit to close the rotary cutter every time you put it down to avoid getting cut as you grab for it. Put the cutter away when it's not in use. Rotary cutters come in three sizes: 28 mm, 45 mm (the most convenient size), and 60 mm.

The cutting mat protects your table top from the sharp rotary cutter. A 1" (2.5 cm) grid is printed on the mat to help you cut with accuracy. Choose a mat that is at least 18" × 24" (45.7 × 61cm), to fit a folded width of fabric.

Clear acrylic rulers come in many shapes and sizes, but a

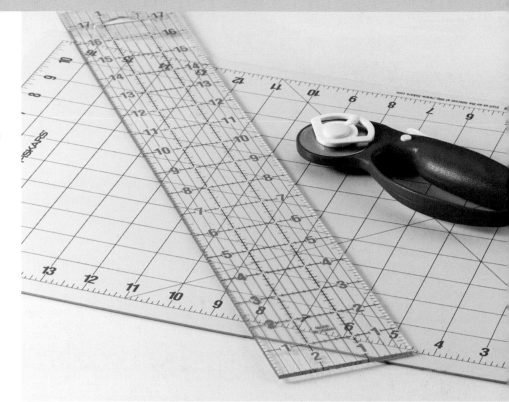

6" × 24" (15 × 61 cm) is most convenient. Clear acrylic rulers used for rotary cutting have printed grids or lines in various increments, generally 1/8" (3 mm) to 1" (2.5 cm). The ruler helps you find and cut the exact size you need. Line up the ruler with the markings on the mat to keep the ruler in the correct position. Roll the rotary blade against the ruler to cut a straight line. Before buying, look at the selection of rulers and find the most readable. (For more about rotary cutting, see page 44.)

Not all projects can be cut with rotary tools, but they can all be cut with scissors. Check the notions section for each project.

here's a hint!

Only use your rotary cutters for cutting fabric. The cutting blades dull after a lot of use. When you buy a rotary cutter, buy extra blades. Change the blades when they stop cutting easily. Follow the instructions on the package.

Carefully discard an old blade—place it in the original packaging or wrap it with cardboard and tape. Even a dull blade can cause damage.

sewing by hand

In this chapter you will discover basic stitches and techniques for utility sewing: fitting your favorite clothes, putting up a hem, sewing on buttons, or finishing a project. Simply by changing thread and choosing some decorative embroidery stitches, you can use hand-sewing techniques to embellish your clothes and accessories to recreate an emerging fashion trend—or to start one of your own.

Threads and Needles

There are a wide variety of threads, in many different colors. Good-quality cotton polyester thread works well for everyday use. Choose this all-purpose thread to hand- or machine-sew seams, hems, and buttons. It is strong and durable and easy to find in many stores. Select a color that is slightly darker than the fabric you will be sewing.

Hand-sewing needles come in sizes that indicate the thinness of the needle. The higher the number, the finer the needles. Sizes 5 to 10, called "sharps," are good for general use. Look for packages with a variety of sizes and experiment to find which feels the best in your fingers.

Embroidery threads are used for decorative stitching. They come in a variety of weights and types (and about a million colors). You can find them in craft, sewing, knitting, and needlework stores. For some of the projects in this book, you'll need embroidery floss. Embroidery floss is made up of six thin strands, lightly twisted together. For fine work, you can separate the floss into two- or three- strand threads. Floss generally comes in small skeins. A skein is a long length of thread or yarn twisted together just enough to keep it from tangling.

To stitch with embroidery floss, you need chenille needles, which are sharp, with "eyes" big enough to pass six strands through. If you are working with fewer strands, use sharp-pointed crewel or embroidery needles. (Sometimes it's difficult to thread six-strand floss, so use a needle threader made for embroidery floss.)

Making Knots

Knot the thread on the needle before you start sewing to anchor the stitches. Knotting the thread is a three-step process. Practice makes perfect.

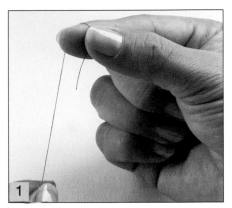

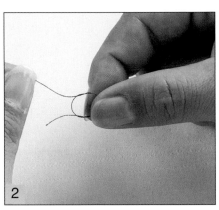

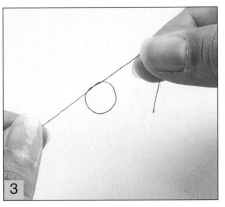

1. After you thread a needle, knot the end of the thread. Hold the end of the thread between your thumb and forefinger.

2. Wrap the thread loosely around your finger. With your thumb, roll the loop of thread off your finger while holding the end of the thread.

3. Pull the ends tighter to make a simple knot.

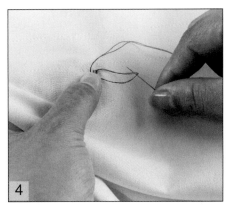

4. When you finish stitching or when only a little thread remains on the needle, make a knot in the fabric before you cut the thread. This knot keeps your stitches from ripping out. Take a very small stitch in the back of your work. The stitch forms a loop. Put the needle through the loop and pull it tight, making the knot. Make two knots and clip the thread.

here's a hint!

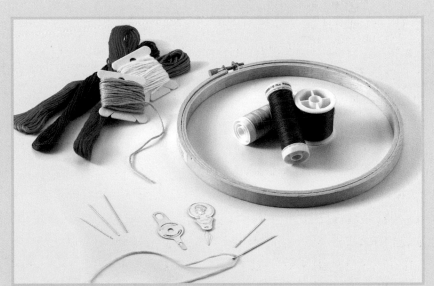

Wrap embroidery floss around a piece of cardboard or a plastic floss bobbin for easier cutting and handling. (You'll find packages of floss bobbins wherever you buy floss.) As your floss collection grows, store the bobbins neatly in a plastic box, basket, or zip-top bag to keep them untangled. Just having a box of neatly organized, colored floss can help spark your creativity!

Utility Stitches

These basic hand stitches give you a good foundation to create the projects in this book. The key to mastering hand-stitching is to strive for even, consistent stitches. This takes practice and a little patience, but the more you sew, the better and faster you will get.

When sewing a finishing stitch on a hem or pillow closure, use a single length of thread (unless otherwise noted in the project). For a single thread, cut a piece about 25" (64 cm) long. Thread the needle (using a needle threader if necessary) and pull a tail about 6" (15 cm) long through the needle. Knot the long end of the thread close to the end.

When sewing a seam or gathering fabric, use a doubled length of thread. Doubling the thread adds strength to the stitches. Use double the amount of thread, pull one end through the needle until both ends meet, and knot them together close to the end of the tails.

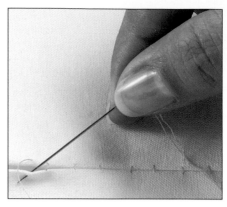

Slipstitch
A slipstitch can be almost invisible—great for sewing seams closed on the outside of your project. Slide the needle under the fold of the fabric as you sew.

Running, Gathering, and Basting Stitches
The running stitch is the most basic stitch and is used in several different ways, depending on the stitch length. Sew straight or curved seams with small, consistent stitches. Make the stitches the same size and distance from each other on both sides of the fabric.

The gathering stitch is a slightly longer running stitch. Gathering allows you to create a rounded shape from a flat piece of fabric. By gathering stitches you can also fit a large shape into a smaller shape (page 25). Basting stitches allow you to sew pieces together temporarily before you make the permanent stitches. Baste with a single

thread. Two short running stitches and one long stitch work well. Baste with a contrasting color to see the stitches more clearly when removing them. You can also baste together the pieces of a garment so you can try it on—no pins to stab you!

Backstitch
Use the backstitch, which is stronger than the running stitch, when sewing straight or curved construction seams that need to be extra strong. The stitches on the back of a backstitch are twice as long as the front stitches.

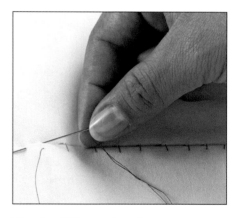

Vertical Hem Stitch
These very neat stitches are made perpendicular to the hem. Work with a single thread and try to just catch the fabric as you make the stitches so they will barely show on the right side of the fabric.

Decorative Stitches

Combine basic decorative stitches to create endless design possibilities. Experiment with different combinations of stitches, threads, and colors. Add hand-sewn designs to accessories and ready-made clothing to make a unique fashion statement. Don't forget that utility stitches can be used for embroidery, too!

Embroider with a single length of thread about 20" (50 cm) long. This length helps keep the floss from fraying and separating. Pull a tail about 6" (15 cm) long and make a knot at the other end of the thread. Be careful as you sew   don't sew the tail into your stitches. Stop sewing and make a knot in the back of the fabric when you have about 6" (15 cm) of thread left.

Many people embroider using a small hoop that keeps a section of the fabric taut while they sew. When you have filled the section with the design, move the hoop to the next section.

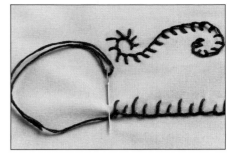

Buttonhole Stitch

Buttonhole stitch, also called blanket stitch, is a great stitch to experiment with. You can use it to hand-sew buttonholes or outline an edge. Try stitching around curves or in a spiral or circle. Vary the look by changing the length of the stitches.

Straight Stitch

Use a simple straight stitch to make an even or uneven row of stitches. Don't pull them too tight. They should lie flat.

Stem Stitch

This simple stitch resembles the backstitch and is a good choice when stitching around curves. Use it by itself or to outline other stitches and design details (especially satin-stitched motifs).

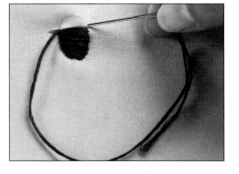

Satin Stitch

Satin stitch describes a group of straight stitches that are sewn closely together to form smooth areas of thread. Work satin stitch only in small areas. If the stitches are too long, they will not lie flat and may snag and pull out. Try satin-stitching with two different colors or with different shades of one color.

Fabric
Scrap fabric

Notions
Container for the base
Tape measure
Compass
Marking tools
Scissors
Needle and contrasting thread
Polyester fiberfill
Craft glue suitable for the fabric
    and the base

pretty pincushions

Every sewing basket or box needs a pincushion—or two or three.
They're handy to have nearby while hand-sewing or at the machine.
Here's a fun way to make a pincushion with scraps of fabric and
small containers—plastic eggcups, condiment bowls, or any type of
round item. Choose a matching or contrasting fabric from your scrap
pile. What a great gift for a friend who loves to sew!

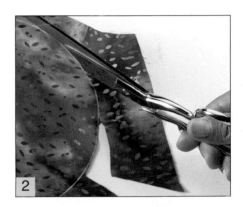

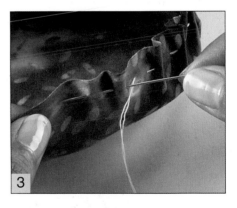

1 Lay a tape measure across the top opening of the container. This measurement is the
container's diameter.

2 Multiply the measurement by three. That
number will be the diameter of your circle. Use
a compass to draw the circle on the fabric, and
then cut out the fabric.

3 Thread a needle with a doubled length
of thread and double-knot the end. Sew a continuous line of gathering stitches ½" (1.3 cm)
from the fabric edge. Do not cross the stitches
or backstitch.

As you sew, gently pull on the needle to
gather the fabric. The fabric will start to form a
little cap. When you have stitched all around
the edge, hold on to the threaded needle.
Do not cut or knot the thread.

4 Gently stuff the cap with fiberfill and tug
the pincushion closed. Place the pincushion on
the base to check the fit. Add or remove stuff-
ing as needed (if the base is deep, stuff it with
fiberfill, too). Wrap the thread around the gathered end of the pincushion.

Push the needle through the gathered end
a few times and secure the thread with a knot.
Cut the thread. Apply glue to the inside rim
of the base and push the pincushion inside it.
Hold the pincushion in place until the glue
grips. Let the glue dry thoroughly.

Size
3½" × 4½" (9 × 12 cm)

Seam Allowance
¼" (6 mm)

Fabric
Wool, 7" × 11" (18 × 28 cm)

Notions
Tracing paper
Scissors
Pins
Needle and matching thread
Marking tools
Large snap
Buttons

Note: Contrasting thread is used in the photography for visibility.

button change purse

Tuck a couple of bills, a credit card, and a handful of change into this tiny, durable purse entirely sewn by hand. It's made out of a firm, tightly woven wool. The snap on the flap keeps everything safe and secure inside.

Know someone with an old jar or candy box filled with old buttons? Add a little fun by stitching a cluster of unusual buttons on the surface of the bag, or just one for a dramatic, decorative accent.

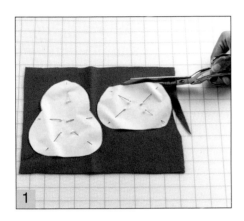

1 Trace the template on page 104 twice—the full template for the back and flap and half of the template for the front. Cut out the pieces. Pin the templates to the fabric and cut out the shapes.

2 Fold over the straight edge of the front piece 1/4" (6 mm) toward the wrong side of the fabric. Sew a hem with the hemstitch and matching thread. Try to slide the needle through the fabric so that the stitches do not show on the front side of the bag. Knot the thread when you complete the hem.

button change purse

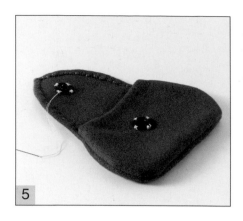

3 Match the fabric pieces, right sides together, and pin. With double thread, backstitch to sew the pieces together with a ¼" (6 mm) seam allowance to form the pocket of the purse. (Seam allowance is the distance between the line of stitching and the fabric edge.) Make the stitches small and consistent. Turn right sides out.

4 Make a ¼" (6 mm) hem on the flap, folding the cut edge toward the wrong side of the fabric. Sew a hem all around the flap, using a hemstitch.

5 Sew the ball half of the snap on the center of the wrong side of the flap. Fold the flap over. With a pin or chalk, mark the front of the pocket where you need to position the socket side of the snap. Check that the correct side of the snap faces up so both halves snap together. Sew the socket half in place.

6 With doubled thread, sew a cluster of buttons on the flap, sewing each button separately and knotting each one in the back.

Stash some cash in
your purse and go!

sewing on buttons

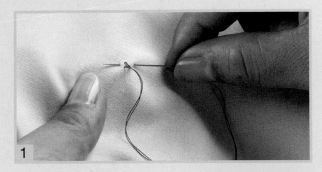

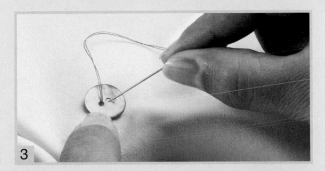

Sewing on buttons is a breeze when you know what to do. Just follow these simple steps.

1. Decide where to place the button. Insert a knotted, double-threaded needle through the back of the fabric. Take two small straight stitches.

2. Position the button. Bring the needle up through the fabric and through one hole in the button. Hold the button down with your thumb. Pull all the thread through the hole.

3. Send the needle down through a hole next to the first. Pull all the thread through the other side of the fabric.

4. Sew through each set of holes four or five times.

5. Turn the fabric to the wrong side and make two knots. Trim away any excess thread.

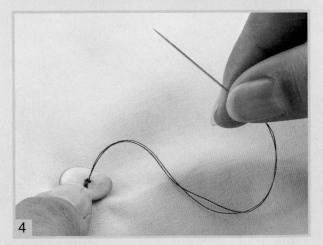

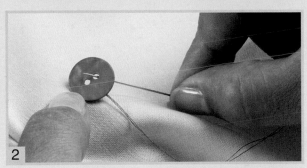

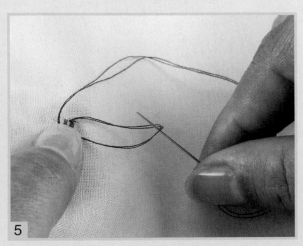

Fabric

¼ yd. (0.25 m) each, assorted cotton
     fabrics or fabric scraps
Denim jeans or other cotton pants

Notions

½ yd. (0.5 m) paper-backed
     fusible web
Scissors
Coordinating embroidery floss
Needles

jazzed jeans

Jazz up a favorite pair of jeans with raw-edge appliqué and simple embroidery. Difficult? No way! Appliqué simply means to cut a design out of one fabric and sew it onto another. Simple embroidery stitches add color and texture to the designs.

1 Cut a piece of fusible web slightly larger than each of the designs on page 105. Place the web over the template with the paper side up. Trace the design onto the paper. Repeat these steps to create as many designs as you want. (If both sides of the web have paper backing, refer to the manufacturer's instructions to find the proper side for tracing.)

2 Iron the appliqué fabric so that it is flat and wrinkle-free. Place the traced design, fusible side down, on the wrong side of the appliqué fabric. Iron the web onto the fabric following the manufacturer's instructions for the proper heat setting.

jazzed jeans

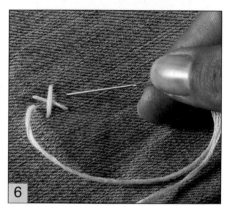

3 Cut out the design with the scissors.

4 Decide where to position the appliqué. Peel the paper from the back of the appliqué and place it, fusible side down, on the right side of the jeans. Fuse the appliqué to the jeans, following the manufacturer's instructions for the proper heat setting. Repeat steps 1 to 4 for each of the appliqués. (You can repeat each design.)

5 Embroider around the appliqués with a straight stitch (page 23), using embroidery floss and a sharp needle.

6 Add straight-stitched "stars" by sewing three straight stitches that cross over each other. Knot and cut the floss between each star.

Jump into your jazzed jeans and impress your friends!

raw-edge appliqué

Often the edges of an appliqué are turned under and stitched. These jazzed jeans have raw-edge appliqués.

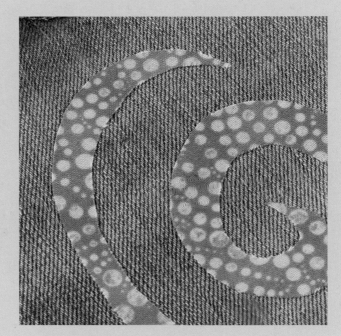

The edges of the fused appliqués will fray with repeated washings—which is just what you want them to do—but the appliqués will not come apart or fall off.

Fusible web is designed to join one fabric to another. You can trace designs directly onto paper-backed fusible web. Roughly cut out the tracing and, with an iron (set according to the manufacturer's instructions), fuse the web to the wrong side of the appliqué fabric. Next, cut out the fabric around the traced lines, remove the paper, and fuse the appliqué to the right side of the garment.

You can buy paper-backed fusible web at sewing and craft stores in packages or in lengths cut from the bolt. There are many fusible products, so be sure to ask a salesperson for help. Read and follow the instructions carefully (for more about fusing, see page 71).

SINGER | Inspiratio

WIDTH

EASY THREADER

TENSION

AUTO

REVERSE

ACCESSORIES

sewing by machine

There are many brands of sewing machines, and they all work basically the same way—although certain features may vary. Spend time reading the instruction manual that came with your machine to become familiar with its specific features.

Look up the basics—how to wind a bobbin, thread, solve common problems, and use the machine's specialty features (such as special stitches and attachments).

If the instruction manual is missing, contact the manufacturer to order one. Search the Internet by brand name and the words "sewing machine manual." On some sites, you can purchase or download the manual for a specific make and model.

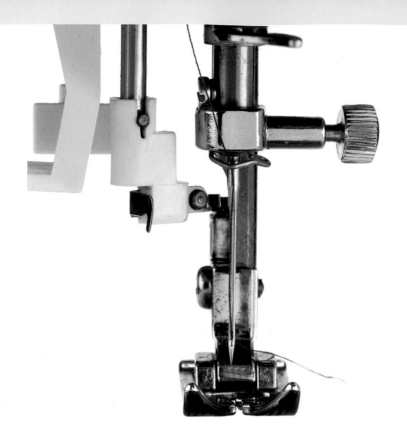

Machine Parts

Being comfortable with your machine makes sewing easier. Spend some time checking out your machine's features—refer to your manual, try things out, and experiment on scrap fabric. Although they may look slightly different on every machine, here are the most basic and essential components.

Hand Wheel

The hand wheel manually raises the needle when the machine is not running. Always turn the wheel toward you. Turn the hand wheel to pull up the bobbin thread before you start sewing or to lift the needle to remove or reposition your fabric or when finishing a seam (the needle is down when pivoting at a corner).

Take-Up Lever

The top thread passes through the take-up lever, which moves up and down in coordination with the needle. The thread also passes through thread guides (both before and after the take-up lever) and then the needle.

Presser Foot

The presser foot holds the fabric in place while you sew. The foot also keeps the fabric in contact with the feed dogs (the "teeth" that move the fabric along). Raise and lower the foot by lifting the presser foot lever (often located on the back of the machine). The presser foot must be in the lowered position as you sew.

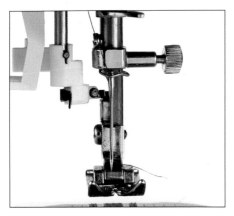

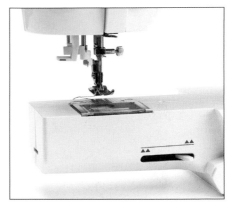

Needles

Sewing machine needles come in a range of sizes. The lower the number, the thinner the needle. The sizes are usually marked with both the metric and standard (American) measurements. The metric number appears first. For example, a 65/9 needle is a very thin needle—a good choice for fine or sheer fabrics. A size 90/14 is an average-size needle, good for medium-weight fabrics. Thicker needles, size 100/16 or 110/18, for example, are best for denim and other heavy fabrics. Change the needle in your machine regularly—it will make a big difference in the quality of your stitching. Be sure to replace a needle as soon as it becomes bent or dull or if the tip is damaged. (Check your manual for the specific instructions for changing needles on your machine.)

Stitch Plate and Feed Dogs

The stitch plate (also called a throat or needle plate) has an opening for the needle to pass through and openings for the feed dogs. It is often marked with lines or measurements that help you keep an accurate seam allowance. Feed dogs are the ridged teeth that sit below the stitch plate and move the fabric along as you sew.

Free Arm and Removable Machine Table

A free arm is a small sewing surface that allows you to slide fabric all the way under and around the machine. It is very helpful when sewing narrow areas (like the hems of pants) and also for some styles of machine embroidery. Your machine may also have a removable machine table that enlarges the sewing surface when the free arm is not in use.

here's a hint!

Keep tools, bobbins, and other small parts in the accessory compartment of your machine or in a small box. Store the box with your sewing machine, so everything that you need will always be at your fingertips.

Machine Controls

Different machines have different types of controls—dials, sliding levers, buttons, or touch pads—but they all make the same basic adjustments. No matter what type of controls your machine has, here's what you need to know about what they do.

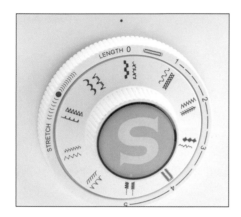

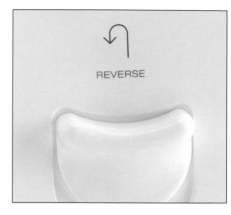

Stitch Length

This control adjusts the length of the stitch. For general sewing, 10 to 15 stitches per inch (2.5 cm) works best. When you sew gathers, the stitches need to be a bit farther apart to enable the fabric to slide easily and evenly along the thread. A good stitch length for gathering is 6 to 8 stitches per inch (2.5 cm). Check the stitch length by sewing a few lines of stitches on scrap fabric. If the length is too short, the fabric will pucker. Lengthen the stitch and test until the stitches smooth out and the fabric lies flat.

Stitch Width

This control adjusts the width of zigzag and decorative stitches (it will not affect a straight stitch) and creates a variety of finished effects. Some machines automatically set the width for a decorative stitch, but experiment on scrap fabric with different settings to see what works best for your project. Some decorative stitches require a special foot, so be sure to use the foot you need. (Some machines that offer many decorative stitch choices may have combination stitch length and width controls called pattern selectors.)

Reverse

The reverse control allows you to sew backward to lock stitches at the beginning and end of seams to keep the seam from ripping apart. Stitching in reverse is like making a knot at the end of a stitch.

Presser Feet

Machines have different feet for different jobs. For most sewing, use the universal, or all-purpose, presser foot. When you put in a zipper, you need a zipper foot. When you want to stitch with a decorative stitch, check to see which foot you need.

Tension and Threading

Tension settings control how evenly the thread feeds through the fabric. If your stitching makes the fabric pucker, the stitch tension may be too tight. If your stitching forms loops, the tension may be too loose. Try adjusting the stitch length first, but if that doesn't make the stitches flat and even, adjust your stitch tension. To get great results when sewing, be sure you have wound the bobbin and threaded the machine properly. You can always just rethread and start again!

Tension Control Indicator
This control adjusts stitch tension. Sometimes very light or very heavy fabrics or threads cause machine stitches to be inconsistent. Check the manual to see how to adjust the tension using this control.

here's a hint!

Bobbin threads always seem to run out just when you need them most! It's a good habit to fill a bobbin at the beginning of every project. Another good idea is to keep a few extra bobbins on hand. Fill them with threads that are the colors you work with most often.

Bobbin and Bobbin Case
Sewing machines form stitches with two threads. The top thread comes from the spool. The bottom thread comes from the bobbin. For general sewing, use the same color thread in the spool and in the bobbin. Each make of machine has a particular bobbin size designed specifically for that machine.

To fill a bobbin with thread, you work with the bobbin winder on your machine. You need to first release the sewing action so that you wind the bobbin rather than stitch. Refer to your manual to find out how to use your machine's bobbin winder.

After you have filled a bobbin with thread, put it in the bobbin case. Insert the bobbin case below the stitch plate, as described in your manual. Some machines do not require a bobbin case. The bobbin simply drops into the machine from the top.

Getting Ready to Sew

Now that you have threaded the machine, practice sewing a few straight lines along the length of a fabric scrap. Lift the presser foot and slide the fabric into position. Lower the presser foot. Sew! When you have made a line of stitching, lift the needle by turning the hand wheel. Then lift the presser foot to slide out the fabric. Gently pull the threads 6" to 8" (15 to 20 cm) away from the needle and cut. Leaving long thread tails will ensure that the needle does not become unthreaded.

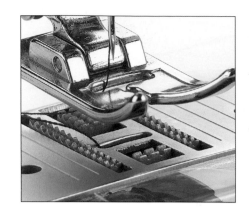

As the machine forms stitches, the feed dogs grip and move the fabric along. Don't push or tug the fabric as you sew—just guide it as it travels beneath the presser foot. Don't sew too fast! If you do, your stitch lines will not be straight, and you may sew over a pin. Never sew over a pin! Hitting a pin can nick, dull, or bend your needle. It can also damage the machine, and the broken pin pieces can cause injury. As the pinned section of the fabric moves closer to the presser foot, stitch slowly or stop stitching completely, so you can remove the pin. Keep a pincushion handy, and insert the pins as you remove each one.

When pinning the fabric, consider how the fabric will be placed on the machine. Position all the pinheads to the right of the raw edge of the fabric to make it easy to pull out the pins as you sew. This way, you will also keep your left hand free to guide the bulk of the fabric as you sew. Place pins perpendicular to the line of stitching and about 2" to 3" (5 to 7 cm) apart.

As you sew, watch the fabric in front of the needle, not the needle itself. Position your hands on the fabric so you have enough control to maintain an even stitch line. Always keep your hands and hair away from the needle and the moving parts of the machine.

here's a hint!

No matter what type of sewing machine you work with—or how old it is—the most important consideration is keeping it in good working order. If the machine hasn't been used for a while, have it checked, cleaned, and oiled. Your local fabric or crafts store may be able to suggest someone who can do the work for you.

stitching
simple shapes

Even though the shapes are simple, the finished look can still be sophisticated. You'll be surprised at what you can make just by arranging squares and rectangles in a creative way.

Working with the Seam Allowance

The seam allowance is the amount of fabric between your stitching line and the raw edge of the fabric. It's very important to keep your seam allowances even and accurate so the pieces of your project fit together after they're sewn.

The width of the seam allowance depends on the project. Garments typically require a ⅝" (1.5 cm) seam allowance. Accessories for the home need a smaller, ½" (1.3 cm) seam allowance. The specific seam allowances for all projects in this book are listed with the project instructions.

here's a hint!

Painter's tape is a great addition to your sewing basket. It lifts off of most fabrics and your machine easily, without leaving a sticky surface. You can find painter's tape in hardware or paint supply stores.

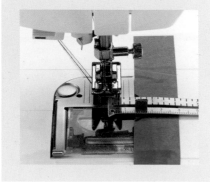

Tricks for Accuracy

Stitch accurately by marking your seam allowances on the wrong side of the fabric before you sew. Lay a transparent, straightedge ruler over the raw edge of the fabric and position it to allow for the correct seam allowances. Mark the line with a fabric marking pencil or chalk.

While you are sewing, the lines on the stitch plate help you maintain a consistent seam allowance. Guide the raw edge of the fabric along the line that corresponds to the measurement for your seam allowance.

If the stitch plate doesn't have marks or if the marks are not labeled, create a guideline with tape. Measure the correct distance from the needle with a seam gauge. Apply a long piece of tape to the stitch plate at that measurement to mark the guideline. Line up the raw edge of the fabric against the tape as you stitch to maintain an accurate seam allowance.

Working with Rotary Tools

When a project calls for a simple geometric shape, all you need are your rotary tools and the shape's dimensions. These directions are for the right-handed person. If you are left-handed, change the blade in your cutter to the other side and reverse these directions. Before starting, read all the instructions. Before cutting the fabric for a project, practice on a large piece of scrap fabric until you feel comfortable and secure with the tools and your cutting is accurate.

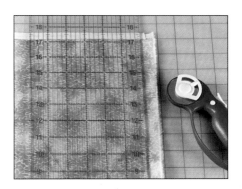

Prepare the Fabric

Iron the fabric before cutting. Fold the fabric in half, selvage to selvage, smoothing the fabric to keep it flat (the selvages will not match perfectly). Fold the fabric in half again. The fabric is now folded in fourths. Place it on the gridded cutting mat with the fold near you and the bulk of the fabric to your left. The right raw edge will be uneven. Line up the fold with the horizontal grid line closest to you.

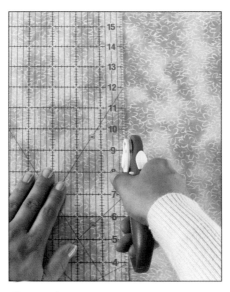

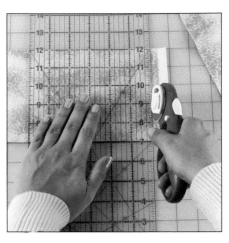

Clean-Cut the Edges

With the first cut, you will trim the fold-ed fabric to create a clean, straight edge, from which you can make all your other cuts. Lay the ruler on the fabric to the left of the right raw edges. Line up the ruler's horizontal edge along the fold. The vertical edge of the ruler should line up with a verti-cal line on the gridded mat.

Stand while you cut. Place your left hand in the middle of the ruler, well away from the path of the cutting blade, and apply firm downward pres-sure. Position the rotary cutter against the vertical edge of the ruler, just below the fold of the fabric. Apply pressure to the cutter and begin to roll the blade away from you along the entire length of the fabric.

If the ruler slips or shifts while you are cutting, lift the cutter, realign the ruler, and reposition your hand farther up on the ruler. Apply pressure again and continue cutting. Check the fabric against a vertical gridline on the mat to be sure the cut is straight. If it's not, line up the ruler again and recut. Always move the blade away from you.

Cut a Strip

Carefully turn the fabric so the newly cut edge is on your left and the bulk of the fabric is on your right. Try to avoid disturbing the newly cut edge. Position the fabric with the vertical and horizontal edges lined up with the gridlines on the mat, as before, to be sure you cut a straight edge.

Measure the dimensions, both the length and width, of your project pieces. Compare these measurements to your fabric. Plan ahead so you can cut all the shapes you need without wasting any fabric. Position the ruler and cut the first strip to the width you need.

here's a hint!

If your ruler is too narrow, use the numbers on the gridded mat to find the dimension you need for the shape and place the ruler on that line.

Clean-Cut the Strips

Before cross-cutting the strips to size, you will have to make a clean cut on one end of the strip to create a right angle. Open the strip. Turn it so that the bulk of fabric is on the left. Line up the strip with a horizontal line on the mat. Line up the ruler on a vertical line. Cut off just enough fabric to make a clean, straight edge.

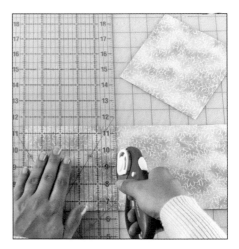

Cross-Cut the Strips

Turn the fabric strip so that the bulk of it is on your right. Measure and cut the length you need to make the finished shape. When you become comfortable with cutting, you will be able to stack two or three strips and cut them all at the same time.

Size

16" (40.5 cm) square

Seam Allowance

½" (1.3 cm) seam allowance,
    included in cut size

Fabric

½ yd. (0.5 m) muslin
¼ yd. (0.25 m) each of 5 or 6
    coordinating fabrics for front
    of pillow
½ yd. (0.5 m) fabric for back of pillow

Notions

Rotary cutting tools
Marking tools
Pins
Contrasting threads
Pillow form, 16" (40.5 cm) square

Cutting List

Muslin, 17" (43 cm) square
Backing fabric, 17" (43 cm) square
Remaining fabrics

off-kilter pillow

This fun and funky pillow will help you master rotary cutting and learn how to mark exact sewing seam allowances. Embellish it with decorative stitches on your sewing machine or by hand. Muslin (lightweight cotton) is the foundation fabric, which allows easier handling of the quirky fabric shapes. Add spark by choosing fabrics with different size prints in a range of coordinating colors.

here's a hint!

Mix up all your strips in a pile or a basket and grab them in random order. It's fun to let the colors and patterns arrange themselves.

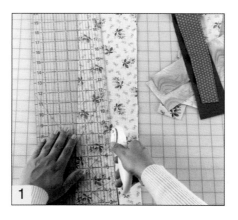

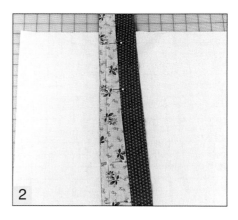

1 Cut out the muslin and back squares. Cut two to four strips of each coordinating fabric 20" × 5" (51 × 12.5 cm). Cut strips from any remaining backing fabric, too. Stack a few of the strips on top of each other. Working with the ruler and rotary cutter, make a diagonal cut along the length of the fabric stack. The narrowest end of the diagonal strip should be at least 1" (2.5 cm) wide. Stack another group of strips and make a slightly different diagonal cut. Repeat until all the fabric strips are diagonally cut.

2 Place one strip right side up in the middle of the muslin square (it will extend over the edges of the muslin). Lay another diagonal strip on top of it, right sides together, matching one long raw edge. Mark a $\frac{1}{2}$" (1.3 cm) seam allowance with chalk or a marking pencil (page 44). Pin, then sew along the marked line through all three fabrics.

off-kilter pillow

3

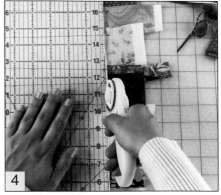

4

5

3   Turn the top strip over, so both strips are right side up, and press flat. Lay the next strip right side down on the raw edge of one of the other strips. Mark the seam allowance. Pin and sew the strip. Turn and press open. Working from the middle of the square to the sides, continue to add strips until the muslin is covered.

4   Turn the square over. Trim the edges of the strips flush with the edges of the muslin square using the ruler and rotary cutter. The top of your pillow is complete.

5   Now is a good time to experiment with decorative stitches. Test them on scrap fabric before stitching the pillow top. Use a contrasting thread and try several different stitches. Be sure to use the proper machine foot for the stitch chosen. Try some hand embroidery or embellishments, too.

6   Pin the pillow top to the pillow backing, right sides together. The raw edges will line up. Backstitch at the beginning and end of the stitching. Sew around the pillow with a ½" (1.3 cm) seam allowance. Leave an 8" (20.5 cm) opening in one side. Trim the corners. Turn the pillow right side out, gently push out the corners, and press. Insert the pillow form. Pin the opening and slip-stitch it closed.

pivoting at corners

Sewing square corners is easy when you follow these few steps.

1. Mark all the seam allowances. Stop sewing where the two lines intersect. Turn the hand wheel toward you to bring the needle all the way down into the fabric.

2. Lift the presser foot and pivot the fabric 90 degrees. Drop the presser foot and continue sewing. (Do not ever sew with the presser foot up.)

3. After you finish sewing, carefully trim each corner, close to the stitching. Trimming helps the corner lie flat. Do not cut through the stitching.

Size
12" × 62" (30.5 × 158 cm)

Seam Allowance
½" (1.3 cm)

Fabric
1¾ yd. (1.6 m) each, two fabrics,
    45" (115 cm) wide

Notions
Pins
Matching thread
Painter's tape

Cutting List
Both fabrics, 23" × 63" (58 × 160 cm)
Mark the cutting lines on the fabric
    before cutting with scissors.
    Measure with the ruler and mat
    when cutting with a rotary cutter.

silky prom wrap

This luxurious wrap is perfect for any formal occasion—and it's simple to make! Just cut out the fabric and sew one seam. The silky apparel fabrics in complementary colors make it special. Contrasting fabrics would be beautiful, too.

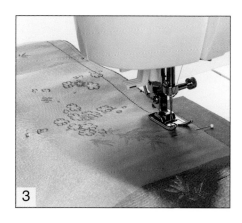

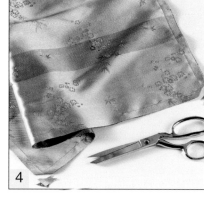

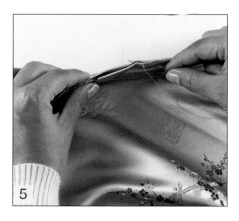

1 Pin the pieces, right sides together, every 3" (7.5 cm) on all sides. If your fabric is slippery, watch to make sure the edges match as you pin.

2 This project offers a good chance to use the painter's tape trick to help sew a consistent ¹/₂" (1.3 cm) seam allowance (page 44). Because the fabric is long and slippery, fold it loosely in your lap before you sew to keep the fabric flowing smoothly through the machine. If the fabric is hanging free or off to the side, the weight of the fabric will make it harder to handle.

3 Start sewing at a short end of the rectangle, pivot at each corner, and sew around the piece, stopping 5" (12.5 cm) before the point where you began. Keep the raw edge of the fabric lined up with the edge of the tape as you stitch.

4 Trim the corners. Set your iron on a low heat setting, and test the setting on scrap to be sure you won't burn the fabric. Reach through the unstitched opening and turn the wrap right sides out. Push out all four corners. Press around all sides to make crisp edges.

5 With a single thread, slip-stitch by hand to close the opening.

6 Lay the wrap on a table. Fold one long side over 4¹/₂" (11.5 cm), and pin it along one short end. Fold and pin the other long side. Turn the wrap to fold and pin the other short end. Slip-stitch the four folds. You are done! When you wear the wrap, the top fold forms a contrasting collar, and both fabrics are visible from the back.

Have fun at the party!

working with curves and trims

Great shapes come from great curves! Master the tricks in this chapter, and your curved seams will fit together smoothly. Adding a simple trim or embellishment also makes a big impact on even the simplest project.

Sewing and craft stores offer ribbons and trims in many sizes and colors. Before buying, consider how the trim will look on your project. Sometimes a splash of a contrasting color or texture makes a big difference.

Consider how the trim fits the use of your project. A nonwashable trim moves a washable garment into the dry-cleaning category. Satin, brocade, grosgrain ribbons, and some laces lie flat against fabric and can be easily topstitched or edge-stitched. Sometimes trims are set inside the seams (which is called insetting). *The Photo Album Pillow* (page 54) treats rickrack trim wiht topstitching and insetting.

Size
12" (30.5 cm) square

Seam Allowance
½" (1.3 cm)

Fabric
½ yd. (0.5 m) cotton fabric,
    42" (107 cm) – 45" wide (115 cm)

Notions
Photograph (print or electronic image)
Sew-in, cotton photo-printing fabric
Cutting tools
Marking tools
Pins
Matching thread
3 yd. (2.75 m) rickrack, ¾" (1.9 cm)
    wide
Wooden chopstick or pencil
Pillow form, 12" (30.5 cm) square

Cutting List
Two 13" (33 cm) squares

Note: Contrasting thread is used
in the photograph for visibility.
Construct the project with matching
thread.

photo album pillows

With a computer and printer, printing photos onto fabric is easy. Add trim to turn your favorite pictures into a one-of-a-kind pillow. It's hard to stop with just one, so make a few. They're fun to have around and make great gifts, especially if the photo is a memento from a favorite vacation or party. The rickrack trim "frames" the photo and the pillow edges. Or you can use a wide ribbon for the frame instead.

printing photos onto fabric

It's fun and easy to print photos onto fabric.

You can print any computer image or photograph that has been copied or scanned. Before printing, color-correct, crop, or resize to get the image just the way you want it.

Check your image by printing on paper first. Then print it onto the photo-printing fabric. These thin sheets of fabric-backed paper fit in the paper tray of any home printer or copier. Look for a "sew in" sheet rather than iron-on or stick-on. The *Photo Album Pillows* were made with a washable and colorfast cotton product. Read and follow the manufacturer's instructions to set the ink, then sew it into something unique!

photo album pillows

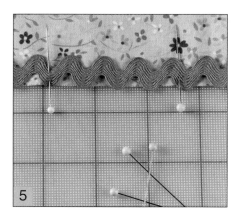

1 Print a photo to fabric following the manufacturer's instructions for printing and setting the ink.

2 Work with rotary cutting tools to crop and trim the printed photo fabric (the rickrack will cover the raw edges of the fabric). If you use scissors, carefully measure, then draw a light cutting line with chalk or marking pencil.

3 Center and pin the photo to the right side of the pillow front fabric. Carefully edge-stitch all four sides of the photo, pivoting at the corners.

4 Measure, then cut four 13½" (34 cm) pieces of rickrack. Pin a piece from edge to edge on the front fabric, covering one side of the photo's edge-stitching. Topstitch the entire length of rickrack along its center. Repeat on the opposite side of the photo and then on the remaining two sides. Your pillow top is done! Put it aside for now.

5 When inset as a trim around the edge, rickrack creates an edging of tiny points. One-half of the rickrack is sewn within the seam allowance. Starting in the middle of one edge of the pillow back, lay the 54" (137.16 cm) rick-rack on the right side of the fabric so that its center is on the seam line. Leave the first 1" (2.5 cm) unpinned, and pin the rickrack until you reach the first corner.

edge-stitching and topstitching

Both edge-stitching and topstitching are lines of stitching made on the surface of a project or garment. Whether functional (to keep an edge from rolling) or decorative (to add a trim), these finishing stitches give your project a professional look.

Edge-stitching is sewn at about ⅛" (3 mm) from the edge of a fold or trim and topstitching at ¼" (6 mm) to ⅝" (1.5 cm) from the edge. No matter which style of stitching you use, try to always sew at a consistent distance.

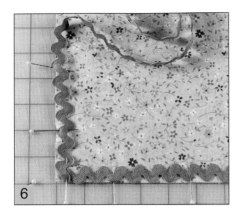

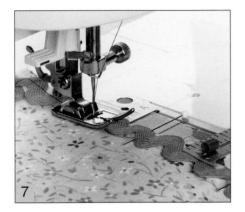

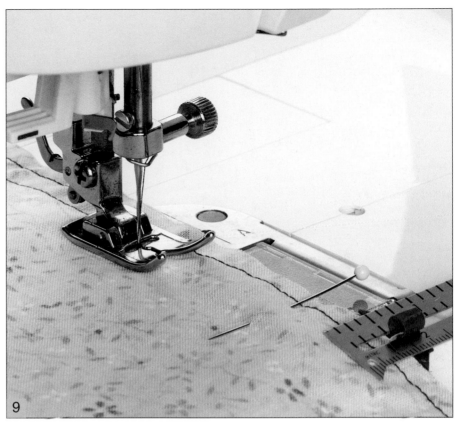

6   Fold the rickrack in a right angle at the corner, and continue pinning around the pillow back. Form right angles at all the corners. Overlap the two ends of rickrack where they meet, and pin, pushing the raw edges into the seam allowance. Cut off any excess rickrack.

7   Slowly sew the rickrack, using a $\frac{1}{4}$" (6 mm) allowance and carefully pivoting around the corners.

8   Pin the pillow back to the front, right sides together, matching and pinning the edges. Backstitch, then sew, using a $\frac{1}{2}$" (1.3 cm) seam allowance. Keep the stitching on the rickrack inside the seam allowance. Pivot especially slowly at the corners where there is added bulk. Leave an 8" (20.5 cm) opening on one side of the pillow. Backstitch at the end of the stitching.

9   Turn the pillow right side out. Push out the corners with a wooden chopstick or the eraser end of a pencil. If the corners do not lie flat, turn the pillow to the wrong side and clip across them. Turn right side out and press. Insert the pillow form and slip-stitch closed.

Start planning
    your next pillow!

here's a hint!

To quickly center the photo, fold it in fourths, and mark the folds with pins. Do the same with the fabric square. Center the photo on the fabric by lining up the pins with a ruler. When the photo is centered, pin it to the fabric. Gently iron out any creases.

Size
Approximately 13" × 13" (33 × 33 cm)

Seam Allowance
½" (1.3 cm)

Fabric
½ yd. (0.5 m) light- to middle-weight
    home decorating fabric

Notions
Pins
Scissors
Marking tools
1 yd. (0.95 m) ribbon, 1" (2.5 cm)
    wide
Matching thread
Polyester fiberfill

Note: Contrasting thread is used
in the photography for visibility.
Construct the project with matching
thread.

Cutting List
Cut the ribbon into two equal pieces.

cross my heart pillow

This witty heart pillow will add style to your bed or sofa. Home decorating fabric and beautiful ribbon give the pillow a sophisticated look. It has only two seams, but they are curved to give the pillow its rounded belly. Sewing supple curves is easy with careful cutting and a few sewing and finishing tricks.

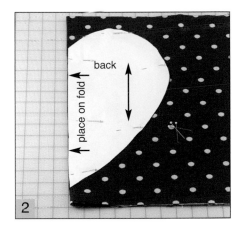

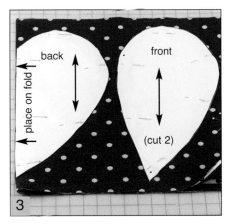

1 Trace the templates on pages 106 and 107, including the dots and the front and back designations. Enlarge on a photocopier. Cut out the paper templates, following the drawn lines. (The ½" (1.3 cm) seam allowance is included in the enlarged size.)

2 Fold the fabric across its length. Lay the back template fold line directly on the fabric fold. Pin in place. Cut with a scissors, following the template.

3 Place the front template on the folded fabric, but not on a fold line. Pin in place and cut with a scissors, following the template. With the template pinned to the paper, transfer the two dots to the fabric with a marking pencil or chalk.

4 Unpin the template from the front fabric pieces. Keeping the edges matched, pin the pieces together at both dots. Slowly sew a seam between the dots, backstitching at the beginning and the end of the seam, and keeping the seam allowance consistent.

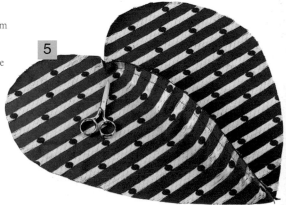

5 Open the front, wrong side up. The center seam will not lie flat, as the curved seam creates the rounded belly of the heart. Clip a V into the seam allowance at each end of the stitching with a small scissors or the tip of your shears, to help the fold lie flat. Avoid clipping into the stitching or you will have a hole in your pillow. Set the front aside.

cross my heart pillow

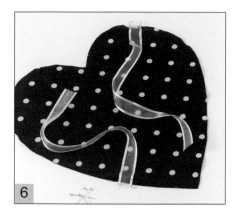

6 Unpin and unfold the back fabric, and lay it right side up. Place a piece of ribbon on the upper curve of one side of the heart. Place the other piece of ribbon on the lower curve on the opposite side of the heart. Pin the ribbons on the raw edge of the fabric. Pin or tape the ribbons to the center, to keep them out of the way as you stitch.

7 Pin the front to the back, right sides together. Start at the bottom and match the raw edges carefully all around the shape. Open the seam allowances in opposite directions between the two clips and pin them flat. Place a pin every 1" (2.5 cm) along the curves, to keep the fabric from shifting as you sew. Mark off a 4" (10 cm) opening along the lower edge (on the side that has the ribbon pinned to the top curve).

Tie the ribbon into a bow— and take a bow!

8 Sew all around the heart, starting and stopping at the marks for the opening. Sew slowly, controlling the seam allowance as you go around the curves. At the clipped top and bottom of the center seam, carefully sew to the clip, pivot, and push the clipped seam out of the way.

9 Before turning right side out, carefully clip the back seam where it meets the center seam. Open the seam allowances flat and clip the back fabric only. Do not clip across any stitching. Turn right side out, and check the top and bottom to see if they are sewn properly. Turn wrong sides out again, and clip all around the seams. Trim the seams to reduce the bulk. Turn and stuff the pillow very full with fiberfill. Slip-stitch the opening closed.

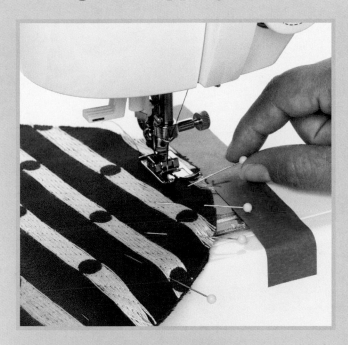

Curved seams allow you to make shapes that straight seams can't.

Curved seams don't require much extra effort, except for careful pinning and maybe some pivoting (page 49). The biggest challenge is to keep a consistent seam allowance while you are sewing. Clipping and trimming seams after they are sewn releases the tension enough to allow the seam to fully curve.

Before you sew, carefully match the shapes of the project pieces. Be concerned about matching the raw edges only. Pin closely all around curves, at least every 1" (2.5 cm) as shown in the top photo.

It's hard to figure out how to keep the seam allowance consistent when a seam curves. A simple guide on the sewing machine, made with a piece of painter's tape, helps you stay in control. For this project, place a piece of tape at the $1/2$" (1.3 cm) seam allowance. Mark a point with an arrow or a dot on the tape. As you sew, guide the curved fabric so that the raw edge butts up to the edge of the tape at the arrow.

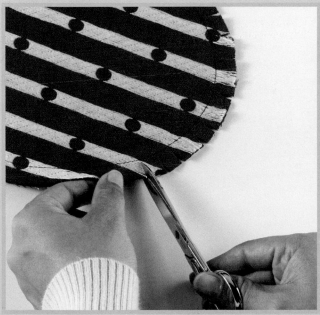

After you've sewn the curved seams, you need to clip them. Clip with a small sharp scissors or the tip of your shears. Carefully make a cut in the seam allowance, slightly more than halfway to the line of stitching, as shown in the bottom photo. Be very careful not to cut through the stitches, or you will make a hole in the seam that will be hard to repair. Clip every $1/2$" (1.3 cm) around a tight curve and less around a wider curve.

Size
6½" × 9½" (17 × 25 cm)

Seam Allowance
½" (1.3 cm)

Fabric
½ yd. (0.5 m) lightweight denim
½ yd. (0.5 m) lining fabric

Notions
Pencil
Scissors
Pins
Tape measure
1½ yards (1.4 m) washable cording
    for the strap
Marking tools
Contrasting thread
Buttons

Cutting List
Refer to the drawings on pages 108
    and 109 to cut the pieces. Cut one
    back piece from both fabrics.
Cut one front piece from both fabrics.
Cut two strips 1" (2.5 cm) by the
    width of the denim (from selvage
    to selvage).
Cut two strips 1¼" (3.2 cm) by the
    width of the lining (from selvage
    to selvage).

frayed bag on a cord

Here's a sturdy little bag with decorative raw edges.
The edges will fray perfectly when you toss the bag into
the washer. Careful topstitching keeps the soft fraying
in place. Frayed lining and pleated bands peek out
around the bag. Laundry day is coming, so start sewing!

1   Refer to the drawings on pages 108 and 109 to measure and cut the pieces. Mark the fabric and cut with a scissors or use the rotary cutting system (pages 44 and 45).

2   Measure over your shoulder or across your body with a tape measure to determine the correct length for the cord. Add 3" (7.5 cm) to that measurement. Cut the cord to the total length and set it aside.

3   Cut one denim strip and one lining fabric strip into 20" (50 cm) pieces. Cut the other two strips 28" (71 cm) long. Mark lines across the wrong side of both denim strips every 1" (2.5 cm) with a chalk marker.

4   To make the pleated bands, center the short denim strip on top of the short lining strip, right sides together. Start at one end and fold both fabrics together from mark to mark, pinning as you go. Repeat the folding and pinning with the long strips.

5   Position the short band 1¼" (3.2 cm) away from the right raw edge of the front piece, and pin it down the length. Position the long band 1¼" (3.2 cm) away from the left edge of the back piece, and pin it down the length. Do not disturb the pins holding the pleats in place. It's okay if the folded pieces hang off the edges.

Be sure that the band on the back meets the band on the front when the flap is folded.

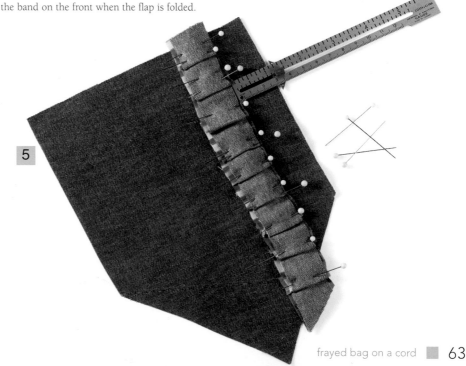

6 Sew down the middle of each pleated band to secure it to the bag piece. Stitch slowly and remove pins as you sew. Match and pin the lining pieces to the back and front pieces, wrong sides together. Sew them together with a ½" (1.3 cm) seam allowance, pivoting at the corners and sewing across the pleated bands.

7 With lining sides together, match and pin together the front and the back sections of the bag. Sandwich an end of the cording between the front and back sections near the top edge of each side.

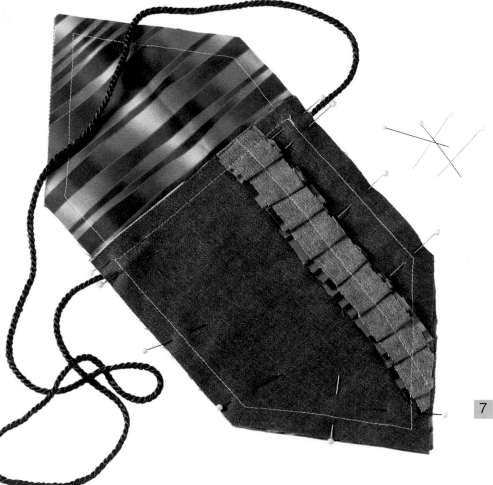

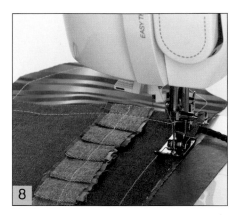

8 Sew the front piece to the back piece, starting at the top of the front piece and backstitching. Use a universal or number one presser foot as a topstitching guide, aligning the left side of the foot with the previous row of stitching. Sew around the front piece and backstitch when you reach the other side of the top. Continue sewing around the flap until you meet the beginning of the topstitching.

9 Time to do the laundry! Coil the cording, and pin it deep inside the bag with a safety pin. Toss the bag in the laundry with a couple dark towels or a pair of jeans. Then toss it in the dryer or hang it to dry.

The bag may come out of the washer all tied up in its own threads. Don't panic! Carefully cut away all the loose clumps of thread— just be careful not to cut the cord or the fabric by mistake. Give the bag a good ironing to flatten it out. Run the point of the iron just under the edges of the bands to lift the pleats.

10 Sew on a few buttons, new and vintage, to complete your bag (page 29).

The bag and the laundry are done. Off you go!

stitch to shape

With flat pieces of fabric and a clever mitered corner, you can make a set of cosmetic bags and a large tote to carry them in! A mitered corner is an easy way to give a flat bag a square bottom. The hook-and-loop closures keep the contents from falling out when you toss the bags into your tote.

Not only do the linings look great, they make the bags sturdy and long-lasting. They also enclose all raw edges. The cosmetic bags and large tote are lined with slightly different techniques. You'll also learn two different ways to make mitered corners.

Sizes
Small 4¹⁄₂" × 6¹⁄₂" (11.5 × 16.5 cm)
Large 5" × 10" (12.5 × 25.5 cm)

Seam Allowance
¹⁄₂" (1.3 cm)

Fabric
¹⁄₂ yd. (0.5 m) cotton fabric
for the outside, 42" – 45"
(107 cm – 115 cm) wide
¹⁄₂ yd. (0.5 m) coordinating cotton
fabric for the lining, 42" – 45"
(107 cm – 115 cm) wide

Notions
Cutting tools
Ruler
Marking tools
Pins
Wooden chopstick or pencil
1 yd. (0.95 m) hook-and-loop tape,
¹⁄₂" or ⁵⁄₈" (1.3 or 1.5 cm) wide
1 yd. (0.95 m) pom-pom trim
Matching thread

grab-and-go bags

Mark, cut, and sew these little cuties in a flash. They may be small, but these lined bags hold a lot. Make them in matching or in contrasting colors and fabrics. These directions and materials will allow you to make both bags. The measurements for the large bag are in brackets.

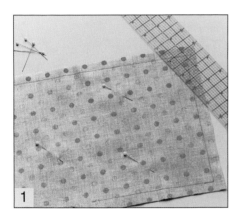

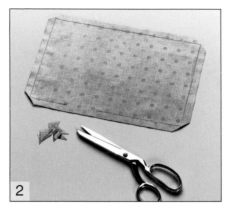

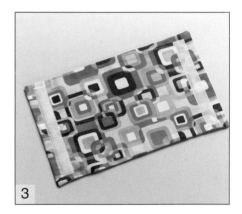

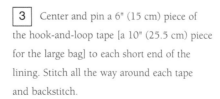

1 Open the outside and lining fabrics and place them right sides together. With a ruler and marking pencil, measure 12" × 8" (30.5 × 20.5) for the small bag [12" × 16" (30.5 × 40.5 cm) for the large bag]. Cut the outside and lining fabrics at the same time. If you are cutting with scissors, pin the fabrics at center to keep them from sliding.

here's a hint!

If you have chosen a raised trim—such as pom-poms or beaded trim—you may have to snip the raised parts that fall within the seam allowance to allow the seam to lie flat. You may also need to hold the trim with one hand as you stitch to keep it out of the way of the needle.

2 Pin the bag and lining pieces right sides together. Sew all four sides, pivoting at the corners. Leave a 3" (7 cm) opening on one long side for turning. Clip the corners, turn the pieces, right sides out. Then push out the corners with a chopstick or the eraser end of a pencil.

3 Center and pin a 6" (15 cm) piece of the hook-and-loop tape [a 10" (25.5 cm) piece for the large bag] to each short end of the lining. Stitch all the way around each tape and backstitch.

4 Cut the trim slightly wider than the bag, about 8" (20.5 cm) [12" (30.5 cm) for the large bag]. Add the trim to the outside of the bag, pinning and topstitching it under the bottom hook-and-loop stitch lines. If you use a wide, flat trim—like a piece of ribbon—instead of the pom-pom, you may need to secure it with two lines of topstitching. Stitch trim only on the front of the bag.

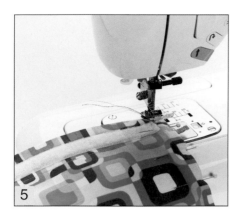

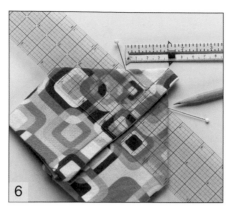

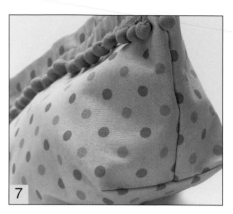

5 Fold the pieces right sides together with the trim on the inside and the hook-and-loop tape on the outside. Pin and stitch both sides from top to bottom, backstitching at the beginning and end.

6 Now you'll sew the mitered corners, one at a time. Keep the right sides together and open the bottom corners. Flatten the corners with your hand. Pin each corner so the seam is in the center. With a marking tool and ruler, measure from the point of the seam along each side of the corner and make a mark at 1½" (4 cm) [2½" (6.5 cm) on the large bag]. Draw a straight line from each mark, across the corner, and pin the fabric.

7 Sew on the marked line. As you stitch, push the seam allowance to one side. Backstitch at both ends of the stitching. Repeat the process to stitch the second miter. Clip all loose threads. Turn the bag right side out.

Guidelines for Fusing

Cover your ironing board to protect it. Lay the fabric, right side down, on the ironing board. Be sure the fabric is wrinkle-free, or any wrinkles or creases will be permanently fused in.

Lay the interfacing on the fabric, wrong sides together, with its edges matching the fabric edges.

Cover with a press cloth. Press for 10 to 15 seconds, one section at a time. Pick up the iron to move it to the next section; do not slide it from side to side. Lift the press cloth to check that the fusing is smooth and the fabric is bonding properly. Allow the fabric to cool completely before working with it.

here's a hint!

Slip an old, clean, unprinted T-shirt over the ironing board to protect the surface while fusing. A piece of parchment paper (found in a supermarket's baking section) also protects the iron and ironing board from fusible residue.

Working with Interfacings

Interfacings add an extra layer to your project or garment during construction. Clothing often has interfacing in collars, cuffs, and pocket flaps, places where extra support or shaping is needed.

Interfacings come in many weights. Pick one slightly lighter in weight than the fabric you are using. Ask a salesperson for help in choosing the correct weight. Home decorating and accessory projects may call for a heavy interfacing, such as craft weight or fleece.

Sew-in interfacings are sewn into seams during construction. This type of interfacing works well with heat-sensitive fabrics, such as velvets, sequined and metallic fabrics, leather, and vinyl.

Fusible interfacings are ironed on. They have right and wrong sides. The wrong side has tiny rough dots that melt and bond to fabric when pressed with an iron. If you are altering lightweight cotton knit, such as a T-shirt, use fusible interfacing to stabilize it and keep it from stretching.

Always fuse the wrong side of the fusible interfacing to the wrong side of the fabric. Be careful when fusing! Don't fuse the project to the iron or the ironing board by mistake. Protect the iron and ironing board from sticky residue with a press cloth. Position the press cloth on top of the interfacing—it will also keep the interfacing in place as you start to work.

There are many brands and types of fusible interfacings. Always read and follow the instructions carefully. They will tell you the proper heat setting for the iron. Check to see if steam should be used or if the press cloth should be damp. Store leftover pieces of interfacing with the instructions so you always know which product you are using and how to use it. If instructions do not come with the product, ask for details before purchasing and write them down.

Size

12" × 15" (30.5 × 38 cm)

Seam Allowance

½" (1.3 cm)

Fabric

1¼ yd. (1.15 m) cotton fabric
for the outside, 42" – 45"
(107 cm – 115 cm) wide

1½ yd. (1.4 m) coordinating
cotton fabric for lining, straps,
and outside pocket,
45" wide (115 cm)

Notions

Cutting tools

1 yd. (0.95 m) fusible fleece

½ yd. (0.5 m) pom-pom trim
for pocket

Pins

Cutting List

Outside bag fabric:

Fold right sides together,
pin and cut.

Two 17" × 19" (43 × 48.5 cm)

Lining fabric:

Fold right sides together,
pin and cut.

Two 17" × 19" (43 × 48.5 cm)

Pocket, 8" × 14" (20.5 × 35.5 cm)

Two straps, 4" × 28" (10 × 71 cm)

Fusible fleece:

Two 17" × 19" (43 × 48.5cm)

Two straps, 1½" × 28" (4 × 71 cm)

reversible tote

This large, lined tote is the perfect beach bag, knitting bag, or everyday grab-and-go bag. The tote features another easy method for mitering corners. A topstitched lining makes the bag reversible and even more versatile.

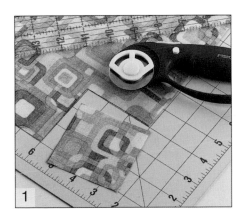

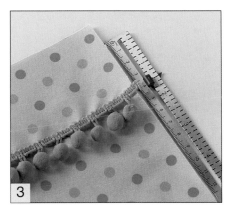

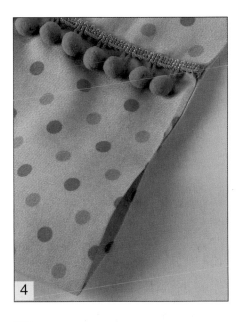

| 1 | Cut out all pieces. Carefully cut a 3" (7 cm) square out of the bottom corners of all six 17" × 19" (43 × 48.5 cm) pieces.

| 2 | Match the shapes of the lining and fleece. Fuse the wrong side of the fleece to the wrong side of the fabric on both lining pieces (page 71).

| 3 | Position the trim on the right side of the pocket piece, 1½" (4 cm) below the ½" (1.3 cm) seam allowance on one short side. Pin, then sew the trim.

| 4 | Fold the pocket piece in half, right sides together, so that it measures 7" × 8" (18 × 20.5 cm) and the trim is on the inside. Stitch around the three unfolded sides, leaving a 2" (5 cm) opening along one of the sides. Clip the corners, turn right sides out, and press.

here's a hint!

Fusible fleece adds sturdiness. Carefully read and follow the manufacturer's directions to fuse. The rougher, shinier side of the fleece is the fusible side.

reversible tote

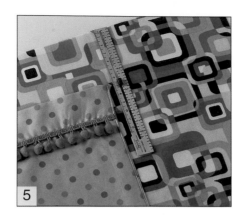

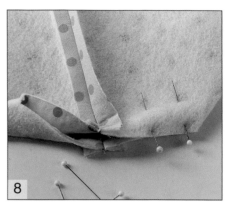

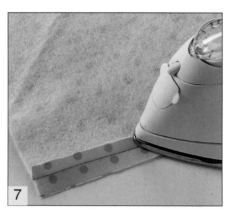

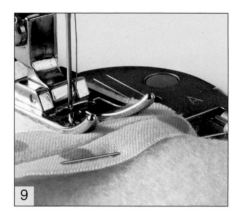

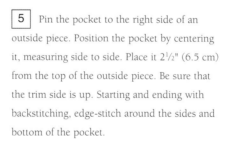

5 Pin the pocket to the right side of an outside piece. Position the pocket by centering it, measuring side to side. Place it 2¹/₂" (6.5 cm) from the top of the outside piece. Be sure that the trim side is up. Starting and ending with backstitching, edge-stitch around the sides and bottom of the pocket.

6 Pin, then sew the side and bottom seams of the outside pieces, right sides together. Backstitch at the beginning and end of the seams. Do not sew in the cutout square.

7 Press the side and bottom seams open. Press a ¹/₂" (1.3 cm) fold all around the top of the bag toward the wrong side.

8 To form the mitered corners, keep the right sides together, and open the bottom cutouts. Flatten, matching the side and bottom seams, to form a straight line.

9 Pin together and sew across, backstitching at both ends. Stitch one side of the bag at a time to make the mitered corner. The bag should now stand up. Sew the side and bottom seams of the lining pieces. Press the seams open. Miter the corners of the lining. Press a ¹/₂" (1.3 cm) fold all along the top of the lining toward the wrong side of the fabric.

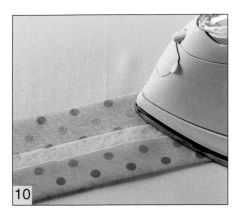

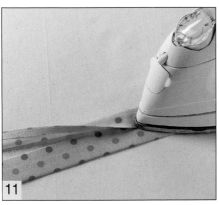

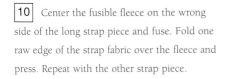

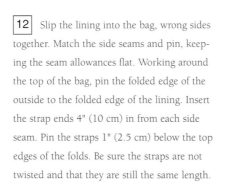

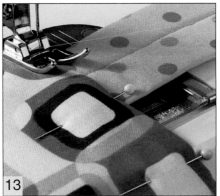

10 Center the fusible fleece on the wrong side of the long strap piece and fuse. Fold one raw edge of the strap fabric over the fleece and press. Repeat with the other strap piece.

11 Press a ¼" (6 mm) fold on the other raw edge. Fold it again to enclose both the fleece and the raw edge for a clean finish. Press, then pin both edges in place. Carefully edge-stitch down the center of the strap, catching the folded edge. Repeat with the other strap. Trim both straps to the same length.

12 Slip the lining into the bag, wrong sides together. Match the side seams and pin, keeping the seam allowances flat. Working around the top of the bag, pin the folded edge of the outside to the folded edge of the lining. Insert the strap ends 4" (10 cm) in from each side seam. Pin the straps 1" (2.5 cm) below the top edges of the folds. Be sure the straps are not twisted and that they are still the same length.

13 Use your machine's free arm, and carefully topstitch all around the top of the bag, staying close to the edge. Catch both the outside and the lining edges and the straps with the topstitching. Backstitch twice at each strap for strength. (If your machine does not have a free arm, be careful to keep the bag as flat as possible as you sew, so you won't sew it closed by mistake.)

Now, grab your bag and go!

working with body measurements

Various brands of clothing fit differently, even when labeled the same size. When you sew, you cannot try things on first to see if they will fit. So we must approach fitting in a different way. The key to making clothing and accessories that fit is to start with your body measurements. When you know what size your body is, you have the information you need to select the proper size for your project.

How to Measure Yourself

All you need to take your measurements is a tape measure, paper, pencil, and a friend to help. For accurate measurements, wear your best-fitting underwear and measure over them, not over clothing. Stand up straight. Hold the tape measure taut, but not too tight or too loose. Don't put your fingers under the tape measure. Be sure to write the measurements down as you go, so that you can refer to them when looking at a project or pattern.

Bust

Place the tape measure around your back, under your arms, and across the fullest part of your bust.

Waist

How high or low you wear your clothes may not indicate your natural waistline. Tie a string or a piece of elastic around the place where your body naturally indents. This is your natural waist. Not everyone has a natural indent, so bend from side to side until the string settles comfortably in one spot. This is your natural waistline.

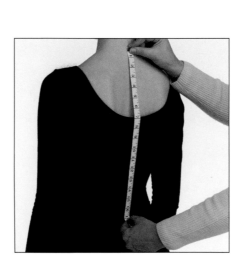

Back Waist Length

Have a friend measure your back from the bone at the base of your neck to your natural waistline.

Hip

Find the widest part of your lower body and measure. Keep the tape parallel to the floor.

how to mark a hem

Put on your garment and your shoes. Decide where you would like your hem to fall. Stand up straight. With a yardstick, have a friend measure the distance from the floor to your desired length. Note the measurement and ask your friend to place a pin or a chalk mark at that point. Pin or mark the fabric about every 4" (10 cm) all the way around the garment. Keep the yardstick straight. This marked or pinned line will become the folded bottom edge of your hem.

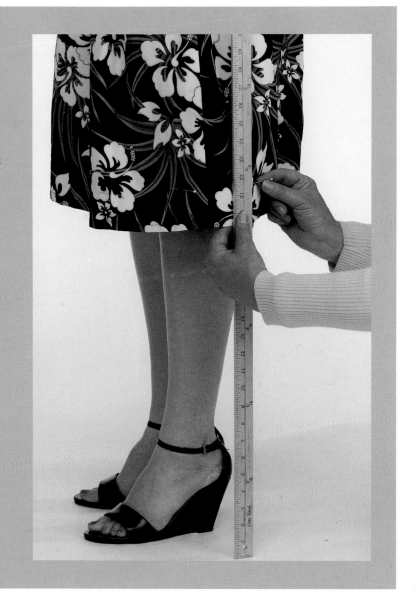

Measurements Plus Math Equals Fit

The *Fabric Belt with Slide Buckle* (page 80) and *Sassy Skirt* (page 84) projects use body measurements and a little math to make simple shapes that fit perfectly.

Fabric

For 45" (115 cm) wide fabric:

Waist/Hip measurement up to
    32" (82 cm), ¼ yd. (0.25 m)

Waist/Hip measurement over
    32" (82 cm), ½ yd. (0.5 m)

For 60" (150 cm) wide fabric:

¼ yd. (0.25 m)

Seam Allowance

½" (1.3 cm)

Notions

½ yd. (0.5 m) lightweight fusible
    interfacing

Slide buckle

Coordinating thread

Pins

Ruler

Marking tools

Wooden chopstick or pencil

fabric belt with slide buckle

Take a measurement, do the math, pick a fabric—and you are ready to make a one-of-a-kind belt to wake up your wardrobe! Topstitching and a great slide buckle are simple details that give this belt a fabulous, finished look.

finding your size

Decide where on your body you'd like to wear your belt. If you'd like to wear it high, on your waist, use your natural waist measurement. If you prefer to wear it lower, on your hips, use your hip measurement. Add 10" (25.5 cm) to the measurement. The resulting measurement is referred to as *Measurement A* in the following instructions.

fabric belt with slide buckle

1   Cut two or three strips of interfacing, 6" (15 cm) wide. Lay the strips in a line down the length of the fabric, wrong sides together, without overlapping. Trim to equal *Measurement A*. Fuse to the fabric following the manufacturer's directions.

2   Fold the belt in half lengthwise, right sides together. Pin to hold it flat. Mark the seam allowance on the three unfolded sides with a ruler and marking pencil. Leave a 4" (10.2 cm) area near the center of the long side unmarked. Pin one short end together and sew, backstitching at both ends.

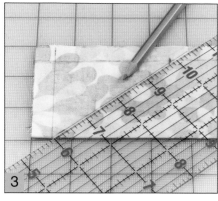

3   Mark a point on the side seam allowance 3½" (8.9 cm) from the unsewn short end. Draw a diagonal line from this mark to the seam allowance mark at the fold on that end. This diagonal line is your stitching line.

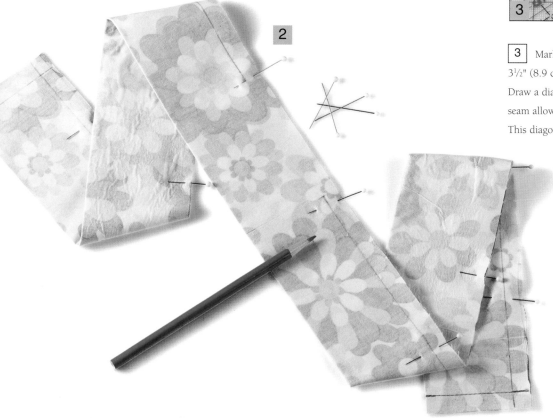

cutting

To calculate Measurement A, see the box on page 81.

Cut one strip of fabric 6" (15 cm) wide by Measurement A.

If using 45" (115 cm) wide fabric and your waist or hip measurement is more than 32" (82 cm), cut two strips 6" (15 cm) wide by Measurement A. After cutting, make a center seam by pinning and sewing the two short ends together. Press the seam open. Using the seam as the center, trim the piece to equal Measurement A.

4 Begin at the folded point and stitch along the diagonal line. Pivot at the corner and continue across the open side of the belt. Maintain a ½" (1.3 cm) seam allowance. Backstitch when you reach the unmarked part of the seam.

5 Lift the presser foot and move the fabric to leave a 4" (10.2 cm) opening in the stitching. Reposition the needle and continue sewing the seam until you reach the stitched end, backstitching at the beginning and end. Carefully clip the corners and trim the point. Turn the belt right side out, pushing out the corners and the point. Pin the opening closed and press the belt.

6 Topstitch ¼" (6 mm) from the edge around the entire belt.

7 Slide the buckle onto the square end of the belt, and fold about 2½" (6.4 cm) of the fabric over it. Place the fabric end as close to the presser foot as possible without hitting the buckle, and pin the fold in place. Stitch across, backstitching at both ends, holding the buckle out of the way.

Clip the threads and try on your belt!

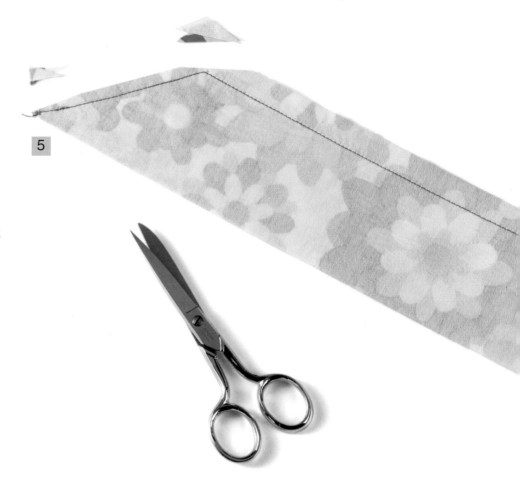

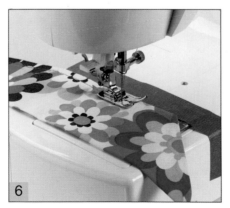

Size

Size varies according to your body measurements.

Seam Allowance

⅝" (1.5 cm)

Fabric

For 45" (115 cm) wide fabric:

Hips less than 40" (102 cm)
½ yd. (0.5 m) yoke fabric
1¼ yd. (1.15 m) skirt fabric

Hips from 41" to 44" (104 to 112 cm)
¾ yd. (0.7 m) yoke fabric
1½ yd. (1.4 m) skirt fabric

For 60" (150 cm) wide fabric:

Hips less than 29" (74 cm)
½ yd. (0.5m) yoke fabric
¾ yd. (0.7m) skirt fabric

Hips from 30" to 44" (76 to 112 cm)
¾ yd. (0.7 m) yoke fabric
1¾ yd. (1.60 m) skirt fabric

Notions

Marking tools
Pins
Thread, contrasting and matching
Seam gauge or ruler
No-roll waistband elastic,
    ¾" (2 cm) wide
Safety pin

Cutting List

(See page 87, "Finding Your Fit," for
    measurements.)
Yoke: Cut two rectangles *Measurement
    A* by 9" (23 cm).
Skirt Fabric: Cut two rectangles
    Measurement B by 22" (56 cm).
Elastic: Cut 1" (2.5 cm) larger than
    your waist measurement.

Note: Contrasting thread is used
in the photograph for visibility.

sassy skirt

Here's a short, breezy skirt you can make, working with your body measurements and a little math. The top part of the skirt (called the yoke) and the gathered bottom are made with two different fabrics. The skirt features a comfortable elastic waist. Choose different patterns, colors, or textures you like best! Get out the tape measure, a calculator, pencil, and paper, and let's get sewing.

■ **measure your waist**
to determine how much elastic you'll need.

■ **measure your hips**
to determine how much fabric you'll need.

(See page 78 for tips on measuring.)

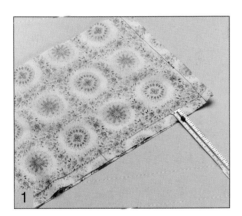

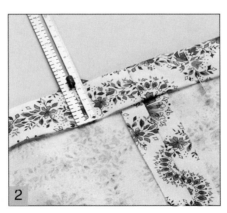

1 Working on the wrong side, mark a ⅝" (1.5 cm) seam allowance along one long edge of each yoke piece (this will be the bottom). This marked line will guide you when you sew the yoke to the skirt. Pin and sew the side seams right sides together, forming a tube of fabric. Backstitch at the beginning and end of each seam. Press the seams open.

2 Fold over the top edge of the yoke ¼" (6 mm) toward the wrong side of the fabric. Press. Fold over the same edge another 1¼" (3.2 cm), press, and pin. You now have a

casing for the elastic. It is helpful to work with a ruler or seam gauge as you fold and pin.

3 Edge-stitch the entire top fold. Edge-stitch the bottom of the casing. Start at the side seam and leave a 2" (5.1 cm) opening for the elastic, backstitching at the beginning and end. This forms the top of the yoke. Fold the yoke, wrong sides out, aligning the side seams so that it is divided into four equal sections. Mark the wrong side of the fabric at each fold on the lower edge of the yoke.

4 Now you'll assemble the skirt. With a ruler, mark a ⅝" (1.5 cm) seam allowance at the top of both skirt pieces, on the wrong sides of the fabric (the top is the longer side of the rectangle). This line will act as a guide when you gather and pin the skirt to the yoke.

4

sassy skirt

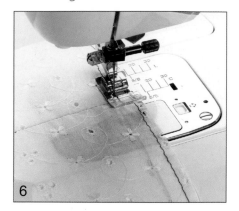

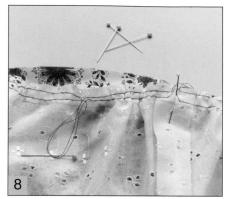

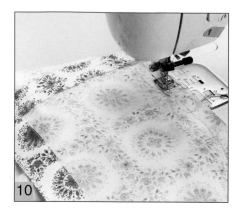

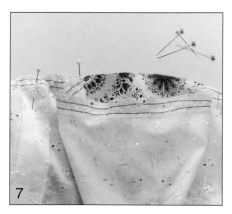

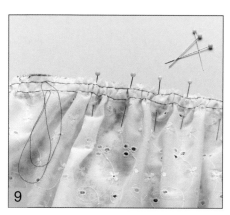

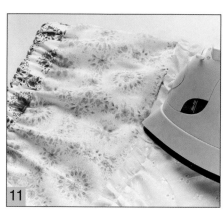

5 Pin and sew the side seams, right sides together. Press the seams open. You now have a tube of fabric almost twice as wide as the yoke tube. Fold the bottom of the skirt in half, wrong sides out, aligning the side seams so that the skirt is divided into four equal sections. Mark the wrong side of the fabric at each fold on the top edge of the skirt.

6 To gather the fabric, change the top machine thread to a contrasting color. Set your sewing machine to the longest straight stitch. Before you start to sew, pull out the top and bobbin threads about 4" (10 cm) so you have enough thread to hold when you begin gathering. Use your machine's free arm, if it has one.

Now baste the top of the skirt tube. Working on the wrong side of the fabric, start at a side seam within the seam allowance and sew a line of stitches about ¼" (6 mm) from the raw edge. Sew a second line about ¼" (6 mm) from

the first line. Do not cross the lines of stitching and do not backstitch. As you remove the fabric from the machine, leave the basting thread tails at least 4" (10 cm) long.

7 Change the top machine thread to a color that matches the fabric, and shorten the machine's stitch length. Pin the yoke to the bottom of the skirt, right sides together, matching and pinning the side seams and the markings on the folds.

8 Carefully pull the two basting threads, working with one pinned section at a time, to fit the skirt to the yoke.

9 Gather evenly, and pin closely, matching the raw edges of the pieces. Ease the gathers along the gathering threads to evenly space the folds. Continue until you have pinned the entire skirt to the yoke.

10 To sew the two skirt parts together, place the wrong side of the yoke face up on the machine. Starting at a side seam, carefully and slowly sew along the marked seam allowance, removing the pins as you stitch. Backstitch at the beginning and end of the seam.

Keep the yoke as flat as possible as you sew and frequently check the bottom layer of fabric to be sure you are sewing only the two pieces of the skirt—not stitching through other portions of the fabric.

When you finish sewing, check the gathering to be sure it is even. If any section of gathers is uneven or if any extra fabric is caught in the stitching, carefully remove those stitches with your seam ripper. Then gather, pin, and sew that section again. Remember to backstitch at the beginning and end of the new stitching.

11 Remove the two rows of gathering threads, and press the gathers toward the yoke.

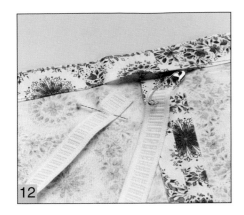

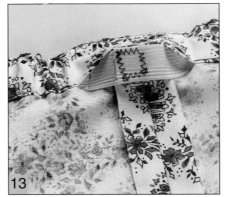

12 Cut the waist elastic to the length needed. Secure one end of the elastic to the skirt. Attach a large safety pin to the other end and push the pin into the waist casing. Work the elastic all the way through the casing, making sure it doesn't twist anywhere. Pin the ends of the elastic together with the safety pin.

13 Now you're ready to try on the skirt. Overlap the elastic ends to adjust the fit of the waist. When you have a comfortable fit, re-pin the elastic ends.

Remove the skirt, and sew the elastic ends securely with a zigzag stitch and backstitching. Hand-stitch the open ends of the casing to close them. Finish the skirt with a 1" (2.5 cm) double-turned hem.

finding your fit

Here are the formulas to compute how much fabric you need for the two sections of the skirt. Grab your calculator and your tape measure. Round up any fractions to the next-largest whole number.

Yoke: Hip measurement + 4" (10 cm) ÷ 2 = *Measurement A*

Skirt: Hip measurement + 4" (10 cm) × 1.75 ÷ 2 = *Measurement B*

Now you're ready to wear your skirt!

making a double-turned hem

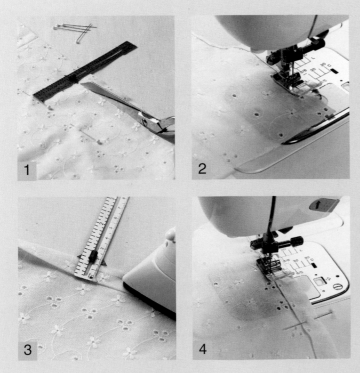

Here are a few tips:

1. Mark the hem evenly all the way around (page 79). A narrow double-turned hem is 1" (2.5 cm) deep. Cut the bottom of the skirt 2" (5.1 cm) longer than the hem-length markings you made. Measure with a seam gauge as you cut to be consistent.

2. Sew a line of stitching along the bottom of the skirt, 1/4" (6 mm) or less from the raw edge. This stitching helps stabilize the fabric.

3. Fold and press 1" (2.5 cm) of fabric to the wrong side. Work with a seam gauge to keep the fold depth accurate, and press as you go. Fold the fabric again, turning another 1" (2.5 cm) to the wrong side. Pin and press flat.

4. Start at a side seam and edge-stitch on the fold, back-stitching at the beginning and end of your stitch line.

change
your clothes!

Editing ready-made clothes is a great way to add something unique to your closet without spending much money. A garment that is slightly worn, too short, or just plain "last year" can take on a new life. Also, the fabric from one garment can be used for something completely different. Just take a look at the *T-shirt Backpack* on page 94!

Before you add trim, consider whether or not your garment will still be washable. Prewash any washable trim or fabric ahead of time, just to be sure.

Once you start digging in your closet for inspiration, you won't be able to stop! All you need is a little planning, a little sewing, and a little imagination.

Fabric
Plain vest

Notions
Heavy paper or cardstock
Scissors
Embroidery needles
Embroidery floss
Marking tools
Hand-quilting thread
Embroidery hoop
Beads
Buttons

embellished vest

Talk about a new look! This plain, black vest needed some color and sparkle. A few embroidered stitches, a handful of beads, and some new buttons really made a difference.

actual size

1 To make the simple designs for this project, trace around bottle caps and jar lids to draw circles on heavy paper or cardstock (a file folder or one of those pesky postcards that fall out of magazines are just the right weight). To make the paisley motif, trace the template at left, cut it out, and transfer the shape onto the cardstock. Cut out all the shapes.

1

embellished vest

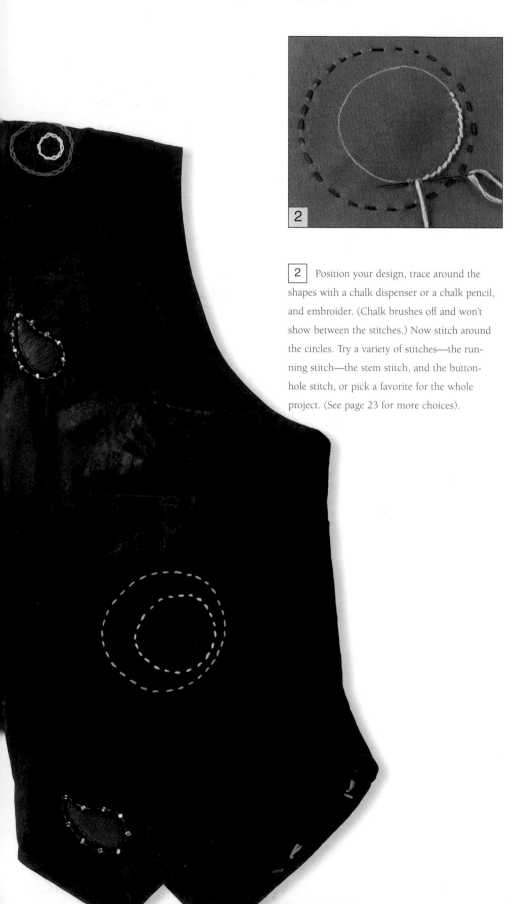

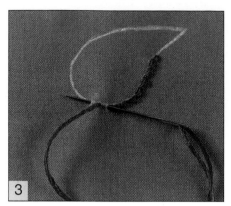

2 Position your design, trace around the shapes with a chalk dispenser or a chalk pencil, and embroider. (Chalk brushes off and won't show between the stitches.) Now stitch around the circles. Try a variety of stitches—the running stitch—the stem stitch, and the buttonhole stitch, or pick a favorite for the whole project. (See page 23 for more choices).

3 Outline the paisley motif with the backstitch, then fill it in with satin stitching. Surround the design with a running stitch. When all the embroidery is finished, randomly sew on a few beads. Replace the old buttons with new ones you like better for a great finishing touch.

here's a hint!

Work with an embroidery hoop if it will fit on your garment. If not, take care not to pull your stitches too tight.

simple beading

Hand-sewing beads to a project is a simple technique that makes a big difference. Use hand-quilting thread, which is a strong sewing thread, and an embroidery needle. If the holes in the beads are too small to allow a needle to go through, try a "sharp" needle (page 20). Another way to add beads is with embroidery stitches—simply slip the beads on the floss as you embroider. Experiment with different sizes of floss, needles, and beads to find what you like best.

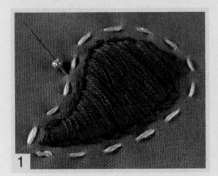

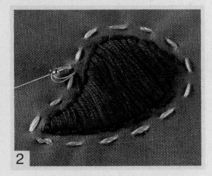

1. Use a doubled thread for beading. Knot the thread, and start sewing from the back of the fabric. Drop a bead onto the needle.

2. Take a short stitch back to the wrong side of the fabric. For added strength, come up through the bead and down again, as if you were sewing on a button.

3. After every third or fourth bead, make a knot in the back of the fabric, but don't cut the thread. Keep sewing. At the end of the thread or when you are finished stitching, make several small knots on the back of the fabric.

Size

13" × 16" (33 × 40.5 cm)

Seam Allowance

½" (1.3 cm)

Fabric

T-shirt

Notions

1 yd. (0.9 m) nonwoven,
    lightweight, fusible interfacing
Seam gauge
Pins
Marking tools
Wooden chopstick or pencil
Safety pin
Two D rings, small
4 yd. (3.6 m) flat ribbon to fit
    through D rings
Tape
Needle and thread to match
    the ribbon

t-shirt backpack

Change a wardrobe staple into a handy accessory.

Turn any T-shirt—a favorite fashion T, a vintage shirt

from a thrift store, or a shirt that you have decorated

yourself—into a great one-of-a-kind backpack!

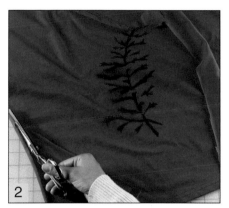

1 Before cutting apart the shirt, measure it to ensure you will have two pieces at least 15" × 19" (38 × 48 cm). Center the front design, if there is one. Use any unprinted piece of the T-shirt for the back of the backpack.

2 With scissors, cut the shirt up the sides and across the sleeves into two large, flat, rectangular pieces.

3 Cut two pieces of interfacing 15" × 19" (38 × 48 cm). Fuse the interfacing to the shirt pieces, then trim each piece to 14" × 18" (36 × 46 cm). Fold and press the top edge (short side) of each rectangle ½" (1.3 cm) to the wrong side of the fabric. Measure with a seam gauge to be consistent. Remember to cover any printing with a damp press cloth before pressing.

cutting and fusing the t-shirt

T-shirts are made from stretchy knitted fabric. Fusing the fabric to an interfacing before sewing gives a little extra weight and stability. Follow the steps on page 71 to fuse the fabric before you start to sew.

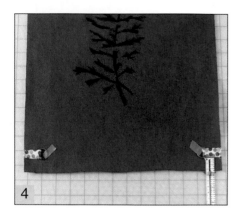

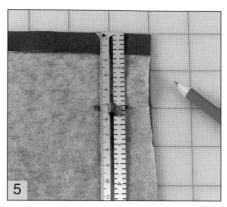

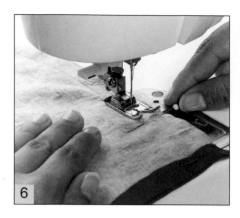

4 Lay one of the rectangles right side up. Measure 1" (2.5 cm) from the bottom corner along the side edge and place a pin to mark. Repeat at the other corner.

Cut two 2½" (6.5 cm) pieces of ribbon. Insert each through a D ring. Fold the ribbons in half, wrong sides together, centering the rings. Pin the ribbons to the fabric at the marker pins. Match the ribbon raw edges to the fabric raw edges, with the D ring toward the center of the fabric. Secure the D rings to the fabric with a small piece of tape to keep them from moving around while you stitch.

5 Lay the second rectangle on the first, right sides together. Place the folds at the top with the ribbons in the side seam allowances. Measure from the folded top down each side, using a seam gauge or tape measure, and mark 1" (2.5 cm) and 2" (5 cm) measurements with a chalk or a marking pencil. When stitching the two pieces together, do not sew between the marks.

6 Pin down along one side, across the bottom, and then up the other side of the rectangles. Leave the top open. Stitch from the folded top to the first mark and backstitch. Lift the presser foot and slide the fabric to align the second mark under the needle. Backstitch and sew down the side of the backpack, keeping a ½" (1.3 cm) seam allowance. Press. As you sew over the ribbon (which is sandwiched between the fabric), backstitch for added strength. Pivot at the corners. Sew across the bottom and up the second side, leaving the area between the marks open, backstitching as needed. Clip the bottom corners.

here's a hint!

Never put the iron directly on a printed part of the T-shirt. Even a shirt that has been washed a hundred times might smear or melt ruining the iron and the design. Always fuse the wrong side of the interfacing to the wrong side of the shirt. Always cover the printed area with a damp press cloth before pressing.

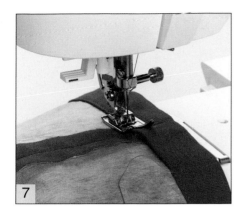

7 Press the side seams open. Turn down the top 1" (2.5 cm) toward the wrong side of the fabric and press. To create a casing for the ribbon, edge-stitch along the bottom fold all around the backpack. Backstitch at the beginning and end. Turn the backpack right side out, and push out the corners. Remove the tape from the D rings.

8 Cut the remaining ribbon in half. Attach a safety pin to the end of one ribbon. Thread the ribbon through one of the openings in the casing, working the safety pin with your fingers. Leave a long ribbon tail as you begin and thread the ribbon around the backpack, and out the opening it started from. Thread the second ribbon through the opening on the other side of the backpack, around the backpack, and out in the same way. Both sides will have two ends of ribbon coming out of a casing opening.

9 Working on one side of the backpack at a time, slip the end of one ribbon through a D ring. Either knot the ribbons together or sew them neatly together by hand. Now there will be a continuous loop on each side of the backpack so it will open and close easily as you pull up on the ribbons.

Try it on!

here's a hint!

You can also make your backpack with fabric instead of a T-shirt. Just ½ yd. (0.5 m) of fabric is all you need. Cut two 14" × 18" (36 × 46 cm) pieces. Reinforce lightweight fabric with fusible interfacing to make it sturdier. The notions and assembly directions are the same as for a T-shirt backpack.

Fabric
Jeans or jean-style pants

Notions
Cutting tools
Seam ripper
Pins
Cardboard
2 yd. (1.8 m) each, two lace trims
Thread to match topstitching on jeans
Buttons

Note: Contrasting thread is used in the photograph for visibility. Construct project with thread that matches the garment stitching.

lacy jeans skirt

Tired of your old jeans? Turn them into a new skirt! Add lace to the bottom for a flirty look. Or you can let the hem fray or add an interesting fabric as a triangle insert. Don't forget to change the buttons, too! Use your imagination and go change your clothes!

1. Cut off both pants legs just below knee length. Set the pieces aside for now. Turn the pants inside out. Using a seam ripper, open the inside seams of the legs. Open from the cut edge of one leg up and then down the other leg. Jeans often have double seams, and both will have to come out, so work carefully and patiently—this will take a while! Turn the pants right sides out again.

2. Open the curved part of the crotch seam on the back and front so that the fabric will lie flat.

how to use a seam ripper

Anyone who sews knows that sometimes you have to rip out seams. If you are rushing or not paying attention, you may sew pieces together in the wrong place or in the wrong order. Or sometimes the seam allowance just isn't consistent enough. Stop working and fix it—it is the only way to get back on track.

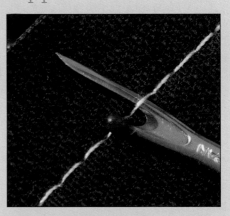

Work the seam ripper on the wrong side of the fabric. Slip the point under every third or fourth stitch on one side of the seam. Be careful not to cut into the fabric. The tiny cutting edge on the inside of the seam ripper does the work. Turn the fabric over, lift the bottom thread, and pull out the stitches. Use a piece of tape or a sticky lint roller to clean up all the little threads. Iron the fabric again to close the tiny holes made by the stitches.

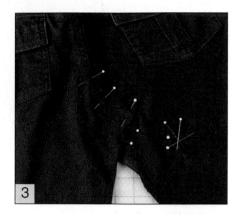

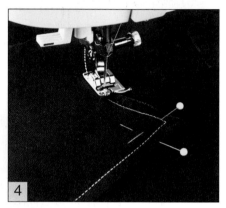

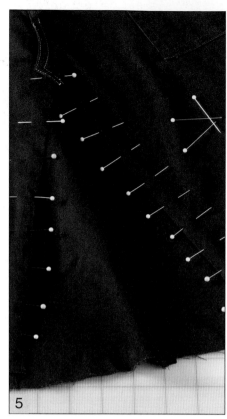

3   Overlap the back crotch seam pieces so that they lie flat. If they do not lie flat, rip the seams a little more. Fold the raw edges of the seams under and pin. Flip the jeans over and pin the front the same way. There will be a large triangle opening in both the front and the back of the jeans. Slip a piece of cardboard between the front and the back of the pants so that you do not pin them together.

4   Carefully topstitch the overlapped pieces together, one side at a time. Be very careful not to sew the front to the back. Generally jeans seams are topstitched with two rows of stitching. Follow the intact stitching lines and match the thread color for a professional look.

5   Cut open the side seams of the leg pieces you set aside. Iron them flat and lay one under the folded seams of the back to fill in the triangle gap. Pin every 1" (2.5 cm). Press. The jeans will have an A-line shape. Be sure that everything lies flat.

6   Carefully sew along the two sides of the triangle. Take care to sew only the two layers of fabric. Flip the jeans over and repeat on the other side. The bottom edges of the skirt will be uneven. After sewing and checking that everything lies flat, turn the skirt inside out and carefully trim away any excess fabric. To finish, try on the skirt, and measure the hem from the floor (page 79). Finish with a narrow double hem (page 87).

7 Pin and sew the lace trim to the inside of the hem so the lace extends below the hem. Edge-stitch another row of lace trim around the outside of the skirt, just above the hem. If a straight stitch does not catch enough of your lace to hold it securely in place, try using a narrow zigzag stitch. If your jeans had buttons, change those, too.

You have a new skirt!

templates
and
illustrations

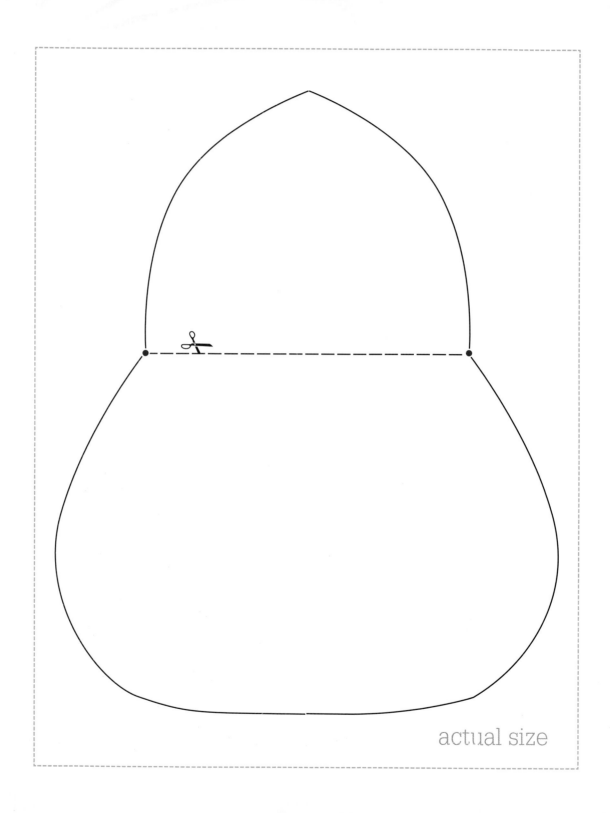

actual size

actual size

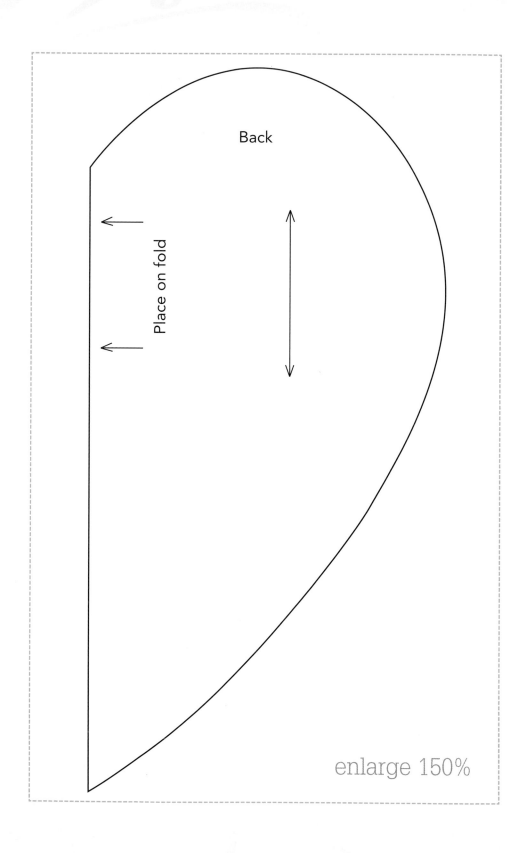

Back

Place on fold

enlarge 150%

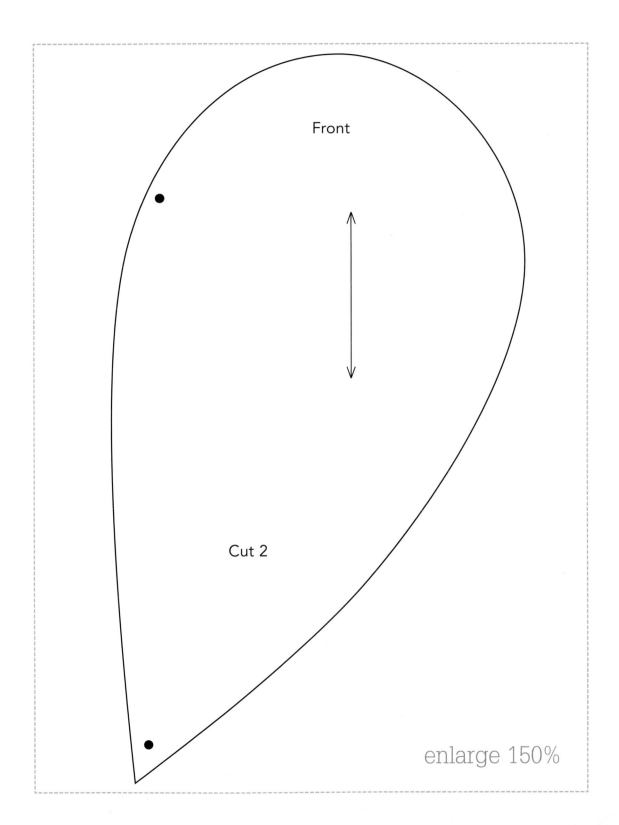

Front

Cut 2

enlarge 150%

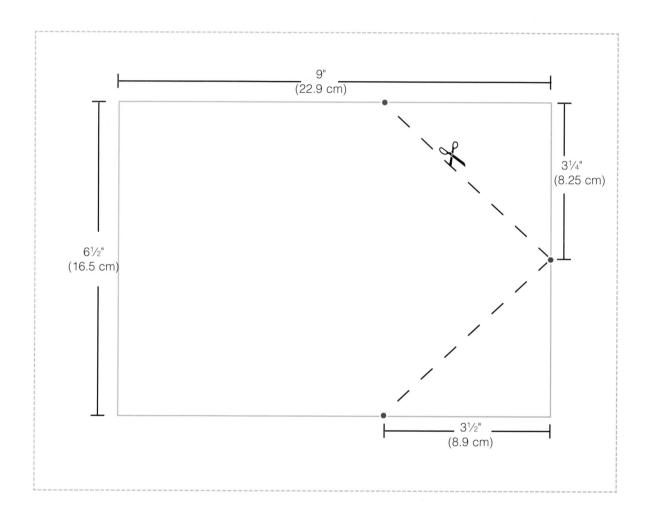

9"
(22.9 cm)

3¼"
(8.25 cm)

6½"
(16.5 cm)

3½"
(8.9 cm)

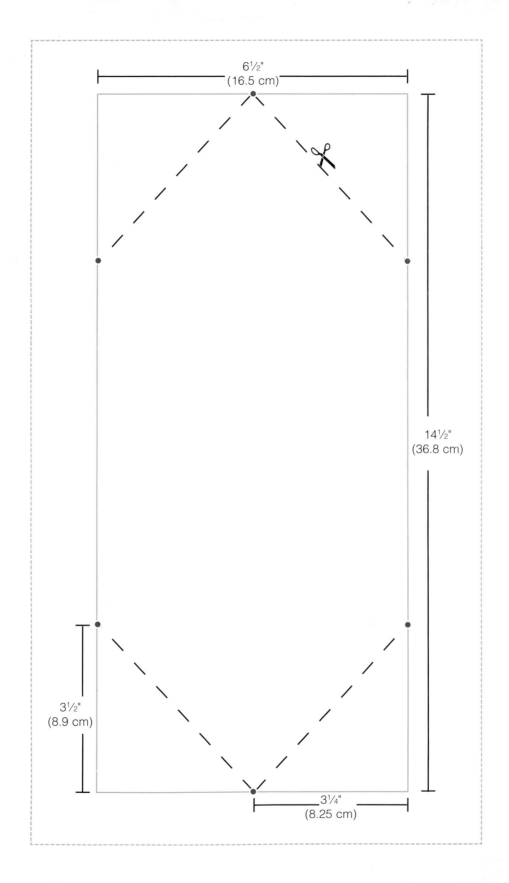

6½"
(16.5 cm)

14½"
(36.8 cm)

3½"
(8.9 cm)

3¼"
(8.25 cm)

suppliers

Buttons

JHB International Inc.
1955 Quince Street
Denver, CO 80231
303-751-8100
www.buttons.com

Fabric

Benartex Inc.
1359 Broadway, Suite 1100
New York, NY 10018
212-840-3250
www.benartex.com

Calico Corners
800-213-6366
www.calicocorners.com

Marcus Brothers Textiles Inc.
980 Avenue of the Americas
New York, NY 10018
212-354-8700
www.marcusbrothers.com

Robert Kaufman Fabrics
Box 59266, Greenmead Station
Los Angeles, CA 90059-0266
800-877-2066
www.robertkaufman.com

Timeless Treasures Fabric
483 Broadway
New York, NY 10013
212-226-1400
www.ttfabrics.com

Sewing Machine and Accessories

Singer Sewing Company
1224 Heil Quaker Boulevard
LaVergne, TN 37086
615-213-0880
www.singerco.com
SINGER sewing machines are
available at authorized
SINGER retailers.

T-shirt Designs

Ben Pasternack
52 Soundview Avenue
White Plains, NY 10606
ben.pasternack@gmail.com

index